To my best friend, whom I have known now for more than half my life. She is a God-fearing woman who has supported me through every single idea that I have talked about or tried. She is an incredible wife, mother, and "grammie." She is a best-friend type of friend to the people she calls "friend." She is my soul mate, and just like our song says, "people do stop and stare when I am with you."

Each person has an idea, a hope, a dream of some sort, which represents his soul. In the long light of eternity, this seed of the future is all that matters! We must find this seed no matter how small it is; we must give to it the warmth of love, the light of understanding, and the water of encouragement. We must learn to deal with people as they are—not as we wish them to be. We must study the moral values, which shape our thinking, arouse our emotions, and guide our conduct. We must put an end to the blind, instinctive, sensory thought and feeling. We must take time to be human.

—William O. Douglas

Contents[ed1]

Preface

My wife, Toi, and I often hear the same question from people: "How did you guys do it?" They ask this in reference to our three daughters—Talita, Tamani, and Tylyn—all of whom received athletic scholarships to some of the best colleges in the country. Our oldest daughter, Talita, was one of the best prep 800 runners in the country, and after several offers from some of the best college programs in the country, she chose UCLA. Our middle daughter, Tamani, although not as highly recruited as her older sister, played softball for San Diego State, where she ended her career as one of the best players to come out of that program, holding several single-season and career records. Our youngest daughter, Tylyn, having watched her older sister's work hard, is currently playing softball on an athletic scholarship at Stanford University, that jewel of schools where academics meet athletics. Three kids, all girls, and no high school drama. All three have achieved a high level of success to this point. People find this remarkable, so they ask us how we did it, hoping to mirror our success as parents.

I wrote this book to show other parents "how we did it," but before I get into that, I need to clarify that we didn't do it alone. We did it with God's help. Our faith in our God and our spiritual walk together are the combined reason for our success as parents—and in everything, we do. This is significant because Toi and I both come from broken families, raised by single moms with a history of family dysfunction. We had to learn our faith the hard way, but harder-won faith is that much sweeter.

Do not just take my word for how faith has worked in our lives. Let me share two real-life examples, and then you can decide.

Living Proof of Unshakable Faith

From the very beginning, Toi's and my relationship centered on faith. We met after we'd both endured heartbreak in previous relationships, and we prayed for each other.

Shortly after our initial meeting, I saw Toi in the complex where my sister lived. I went and knocked on Toi's door, saying, "I just want you to know that we will be together someday."

At that time, Toi's daughters, Tamani and Talita, were three and a half years and eighteen months old, respectively.

From the moment I knocked on Toi's door that day until this moment, Toi and I have been together, and Tamani and Talita have been my daughters too, not just Toi's. Toi and I later had a daughter together, Tylyn. We are a family, now and forevermore.

So, yes, faith has always been alive and at work in our lives. Our meeting was just one real-life example of that. Now I'll share another.

Back in 1996, when the girls were twelve, ten, and three, Toi and I discussed creating a different lifestyle for our family, one we felt we couldn't have in Los Angeles, where we lived at that time. We soon traveled to a family reunion in Atlanta, and we thought we would explore the South as a possible destination for our family. After all, most of my paternal family resided in Georgia, as my dad had moved back to his birthplace when I was thirteen. If we relocated there, I would have two brothers and a sister living nearby. Toi and I had heard that Atlanta was the mecca for professional Blacks, so we were open to considering moving there.

After praying for a sign, we arrived in Atlanta, only to encounter some of the worst heat and humidity I'd ever experienced. I had been to the South many times, but this was different.

While sitting at one of my young cousin's track meets, I turned to Toi, saying, "I can't breathe in this heat. I can't live here."

And with that, Atlanta was off our list.

A few months later we were at Talita's track meet in Phoenix, so of course we figured we would check out Arizona as a possible relocation destination. Like Atlanta, Phoenix was too hot for us (though the humidity was absent this time).

With two potential destinations eliminated, we continued to stay faithful, asking God for a sign.

A few months later, in December 1996, I attended a workshop in Santa Cruz, California, where I met a woman (I'll refer to her as Stephanie C.). Stephanie was looking for a director for her supported-living program in Lafayette, an affluent city in the Bay Area, just outside San Francisco. After discussing the position with Stephanie, I again asked God to send me a sign. I then called Toi, told her about the opportunity, and asked her to fax my résumé to me at the hotel hosting the workshop. (Remember, this was in pre-Internet 1996.) I gave my résumé to Stephanie, and she asked me to come to

Lafayette for an interview.

I quickly scheduled a flight to Northern California. Toi and I prayed before I left for the interview, and I asked God to give me a sign. What I heard loud and clear was that if Stephanie offered me the position, it would be God's way of telling me to make the move. An hour after the interview, Stephanie called to let me know she was offering me the position. I was sure this was God's sign and answer.

Once I was back in Southern California, Toi and I reviewed the offer, quickly realizing the moving expenses would result in our laying out money we didn't have. After a few minutes of praying about it, the phone rang: it was my new supervisor calling to tell me that management realized the relocation package they had offered was probably too low, and they wanted to offer us additional monies toward the move to take the stress off us. Once again, there was God showing up right when we needed him.

After making the move to Northern California, we had to look for a house. We soon discovered the housing market was tough on buyers, and we kept getting outbid. However, God had other plans.

We decided Toi and the girls would remain in the house we rented in Southern California, in order to allow the kids to finish the school year. In the meantime, I met many people whom God put in our lives to help us; each and every one of them would be instrumental in God's plan for us. I'll tell you about the two who, with God's guidance, helped us the most.

The first was Raja, a real estate agent who gave me a blueprint on what we would need to purchase a home in that area. For the next few months, while working on this plan, I prayed that God would lead us to the right house.

Once school was out, Toi and the girls joined me in Northern California. One day while at the park in June 1997, Toi met a man who was playing catch with his daughter. This man's name is Darin Sheridan, and he ended up being the coach I met at the girls' softball tryouts in January 1998, but I had no idea my wife had met him some months prior. We only discovered this when Toi took Tamani to her first practice in April. I got to know Darin and his family, but I had no idea he would help me out within a few months—that was another sign from God.

As the summer season proceeded, Raja and I felt like it was a good time to start looking for houses. After several attempts to make an offer, only to be outbid, Darin informed me that he was a general contractor and, if I would like, he would be willing to check out any house that I was interested in buying to make sure I was getting a good house for my money. So Darin was the second person sent by God to help my family and me—further proof of how God answers prayers.

Early one Saturday morning, Tamani and I were looking for houses, and she asked me to stop at a house I thought for sure was out of our price range. However, I stopped anyway, called Darin, and waited for him to meet me at the house. I called Raja and gave her the address, and when she looked it up she discovered the house wasn't even on the market, which meant it had no offers on it. While I was talking with Raja, Darin wanted to tell me something before I told her what we wanted to offer for the house. I let her know I needed a few minutes and would call her back shortly.

Darin then told me, "My wife and I understand you guys keep getting outbid. We want to help you. We will lend you $2,500, under two conditions. First, you cannot worry about paying us back until you are in a position where it won't be a hardship. Second, you have to look for houses in our neighborhood, because we think you're good people."

Imagine how I felt in response to this man's generosity and kindness. Well, as God would have it, this house was right across the park from Darin's house, and the park was the same one where my wife first saw him and his daughter playing catch. Toi had stopped to ask him where she could sign Tamani up for softball, not knowing he was the coach. When I met him as the coach, I had no idea Toi had already spoken to him, as I've explained. Neither one of us could have possibly known what a key role he would play in our lives. Toi and I had been praying frequently, asking God to help us find a house. God alone led me to Raja, and also to Darin, an incredible coach with a wonderful family. They are some of our best friends, even to this day.

My faith in God was unshakable before he provided us with our house and our friends, and it is still unshakable. That same unshakable faith has enabled my wife and me to raise our daughters in the way that we did, leading to their many achievements and continued success. I hope this book will help other parents like you, with values similar to my wife's and mine, to attain similar successes with your children, and I am excited to share with you what I know has worked. Talita, Tamani, and Tylyn are living proof!

In addition to the true story I shared above, below are my three daughters' individual takes on faith.

On Faith—Or, the Significance of 41/7

[Author's Note: *Throughout this book, the numbers seven and forty-one are expressed in numeral form as 7 and 41.*]

If the above heading seems strange, let me explain that the original title of this book was *41/7*.

What an interesting name for a book, you might think, wondering, *Why these numbers? What is their significance?*

Everyone knows what 24/7 means, but 41/7? Well, that's why I changed the title to *The 7 Principles of Faith-Based Parenting*. The title gives you a clue as to how important the number 7 will be throughout our journey toward parenting successful kids. But what about 41? It's equally important to my family and me, but it does its work "behind the scenes" in this book. People who know my family will easily recognize the significance of these two numbers.

Before we go any further in our journey together, I'm going to let Talita, Tamani, and Tylyn describe to you the full significance of the numbers 7 and 41. Without letting them know the reason why, I asked each of my daughters what significance the numbers 41 and 7 had for them. Their answers appear below, and they will explain not only what these numbers mean to me and my family but also why 41 and 7 are all about faith.

Talita

The number 41 was your football number, Dad. Although I have never really worn a uniform that required a number, 41 has always been a number I've held close. For me, it's not really about the number. It's about who that number represents, and 41 represents you, Dad. The number 41 reminds me of your discipline, your integrity, your faith, your drive, your leadership, your persistence to be your best self and achieve your dreams. You are an inspiration, and 41 signifies that for me. I could be mistaken, but if so, it's only slightly—I think 41 means the same thing for the rest of our family as it does for me.

Similarly, the number 7 is the number both my sisters wore for softball. I am not really sure why 7 is such a popular number among softball players. Perhaps it's the relation to the notion of "lucky 7," and winning. For the meaning 7 has for me, I'll go by what it means in the Bible: God's symbolic number for fullness, completion, and perfection (of his initial creative act). The work God ended in 7 days was the beginning of a gift. When I think of the number 7 in terms of performance, it symbolizes the full execution of your plan—all that you have worked hard for, prepared for, planned for, and visualized must be left on the proverbial track; it's also the number of days/opportunities/chances you have every week to do something great, to make a difference.

Tamani

Dad, 41 is your athletic number—and your legacy. Both 41 and 7 represent our family's drive and accomplishments. I have had some good times wearing those numbers, and I still feel encouraged when I get anything with the number 7 or 41 on it.

Tylyn

I associate the number 41 with you, Dad. That is your athletic identity. Whenever I see the number 41, I think of you. I associate the number 7 with Tamani and myself. That number was each of our athletic identities for the longest time. It is a lucky number. It is the perfect number. And in my opinion, based on the Bible, it is one of God's numbers. I think the rest of our family feels the same way. The numbers 7 and 41 are significant for us because we have deep, long-lasting memories associated with those numbers.

*

So you can see that although Talita, Tamani, and Tylyn each answered my question about the significance of 41 and 7, they also told me their beliefs about family, integrity, success, and faith. And that's exactly what the rest of this book will help you do—and it will help you teach your children how to do it too.

Now that you've read this far, let's move on through the book to see just how much further our faith can take us[MJO2] …

Introduction

As described in the preface, this book is about the tools my wife and I used to raise our three daughters. It details our "secret" to raising three girls who all stayed out of trouble, earned athletic scholarships, and are now well-adjusted, awesome young women. The secret is that it isn't a secret at all! It is unshakable faith in our God. We communicated that faith to our daughters, and they succeeded because of it.

This book offers tools and tips to help make faith work for you. Think of it as the practical application of spiritual belief.

Our girls all stayed on the straight and narrow; they excelled in school and in athletics. We were not rich, but we facilitated their success by using the minimal resources we had. We trusted in our God and relied on each other.

All Christian parents raising their families in a challenging world can do the same things my wife and I did. This book offers insights on what it takes to raise successful kids, as well as tips and tools that you can easily implement in your own life.

To put it simply, and as the title reflects, this book centers on 7 principles. Please understand that each of these principles will mean something different to each of us, depending on where we come from, where we are in our lives while reading this book, and where we intend to go after we finish reading it.

Toi and I have practiced all of these principles in raising our children and in every aspect of our lives. Now I wish to share them with you, fellow parents seeking to raise children who will be grace-filled and well-adjusted by modeling the lessons of faith you have taught them.

The 7 Principles of Faith-Based Parenting

1. Seek the truth, and base your life on it.
2. Understand who you are by knowing your family history and traditions.
3. Be family oriented.
4. Be selective about your friends.
5. Change what you need to by removing bad habits.

6.   Do not fear failure while working toward success.

7.   Always be yourself, but also see yourself as others see you.

Chapters 1 through 7 each will go through the principles one by one, respectively. At the end of each chapter, there will be a set of principle-related exercises for you to complete—titled "Principle in Practice"—followed by a page with tips for how you can teach that same principle to your child(ren) in an age-appropriate way.

[Author's Note: *Please refer to the "Tools for Success" section in the back of the book for even more exercises and resources. You can utilize these while reading this book, after you finish it, and as many times as you wish in the future. My ultimate goal is for this book to become a perennial resource for you as a parent, all throughout the growing-up years of your child(ren).*]

Now, before we delve into each of the principles, let's briefly touch on something that we, as parents, must impart to our children: the importance of having and fulfilling dreams.

<<insert image 1>>

Dreaming SMART

We all may know that it's important to have dreams and to fulfill them. But one of the most important lessons that we parents can teach our children is how to dream smart. Not just smart, but SMART (Specific, Measurable, Accountable, Realistic, Time-bound).[1] SMART dreams are easier to fulfill because they become goals. Realized goals become achievements, and attained achievements lead to lasting success and fulfillment. Understanding how to dream SMART shows children how to set and reach attainable goals, how to recognize the difference between a dream and a goal, and how to make dreams reality—if they are willing to do the work required to get there.

Toi and I discovered early on that dreams were the most powerful tools we could give our girls. We recognized this long before we learned about the SMART system. In simplest terms, children's dreams represent their hopes and desires for whatever they chose to be and do in life. No one can set or reach a goal without first having a dream!

The first step toward making dreams real is making them tangible. Create a dream book using pictures from magazines, inspirational quotes, and your own words and phrases. Let this book guide you to begin aligning what your future will be. You can then encourage your child(ren) to do the same, in the age-appropriate manner determined by you.

Start by describing one hundred dreams using the pictures, quotes, words, etc., that you have collected. Set a goal for each dream. Next, set a timeline for each goal, in order to motivate you to achieve each goal. Also, pick someone who will help you stay committed to reaching each goal. You'll notice that these steps achieve each aspect of the SMART system, as the table below illustrates.

Specific	images, quotes, words, etc., collected for each dream
Measurable	goal set for each dream
Accountable	partner picked to help you stay committed to each goal
Realistic	each goal is attainable, given your resources and within the time frame set by you
Time-bound	time frame established and committed to by you

SMART[2]

Use the SMART System Tracker for Dreams/Goals on the pages that follow as your guide through the process described above. There is a sample SMART Tracker for you to use to implement your own dreams/goals, and another one for you to use to help your child(ren) create SMART dreams/goals in age-appropriate ways. (There are more SMART Trackers in the "Tools for Success" section in the back of this book.)

SMART[3] System Tracker for Dreams/Goals
Make All Your Dreams/Goals SMART!

Specific	images, quotes, words, etc., collected for each dream
Measurable	goal set for each dream
Accountable	partner picked to help you stay committed to each goal
Realistic	each goal is attainable, given your resources and within the time frame set by you
Time-bound	time frame established and committed to by you

Using the above system to Make All Your Dreams/Goals SMART, create a SMART System Tracker that will keep you accountable for progress while living and practicing the 7 principles. The SMART Tracker below will help you get started. Make your own SMART System Trackers to use on as many dreams/goals as you wish to realize.

SMART Tracker

Dream/Goal: _____

Specific	**Progress**	**Week #**	**Result**
Measurable	**Progress**	**Week #**	**Result**
Accountable	**Progress**	**Week #**	**Result**
Realistic	**Progress**	**Week**	**Result**

		Week #	
Time-bound	**Progress**	**Week** #	**Result**

At the top of the SMART Tracker (above), write in the Dream/Goal.

Use each of the SMART boxes to ensure that you create a goal from your dream according to the SMART system (Specific, Measurable, Accountable, Realistic, and Time-bound).

In the Progress boxes, mark a "+" if you were on target and a "–" if you were not on target. This will help you stay accountable, whether you are doing this on your own or with a partner.

In the Week # boxes, just indicate which week it is, to help you stay accountable.

In the Results box, indicate the outcome of having created the goal from the dream.

Repeat the above steps for as long as you need to until you achieve your desired result(s). After that, move to the next dream you wish to turn into a goal and follow the same steps. Use the SMART System Trackers in the "Tools for Success" section in the back of this book.

SMART[4] System Tracker for Dreams/Goals

Help Your Children Make All Their Dreams/Goals SMART!

Specific	images, quotes, words, etc., collected for each dream
Measurable	goal set for each dream
Accountable	partner picked to help you stay committed to each goal
Realistic	each goal is attainable, given your resources and within the time frame set by you
Time-bound	time frame established and committed to by you

Using the above system to Make All Dreams/Goals SMART, help your child(ren) create a SMART Tracker that will keep all of you accountable for progress in achieving set goals. The tracker below will help you get your child(ren) started. Follow the same system you used to complete your own tracker(s), but in an age-appropriate way for your child(ren). There are more SMART System Trackers in the "Tools for Success" section in the back of this book.

SMART Tracker

Dream/Goal: _____

Specific	Progress	Week #	Result
Measurable	**Progress**	**Week #**	**Result**
Accountable	**Progress**	**Week #**	**Result**
Realistic	**Progress**	**Week #**	**Result**
Time-bound	**Progress**	**Week #**	**Result**

[Author's Note: *The following instructions, which are the same ones that appeared with the tracker in the previous section, are designed for parents to use with their child(ren), in an age-appropriate way. They are not intended for children to use on their own.*]

At the top of the SMART Tracker (above), write in the Dream/Goal.

Use each of the SMART boxes to ensure that you create a goal from your dream according to the SMART system (Specific, Measurable, Accountable, Realistic, and Time-bound).

In the Progress boxes, mark a "+" if you were on target and a "–" if you were not on target. This will help you stay accountable, whether you are doing this on your own or with a partner.

In the Week # boxes, just indicate which week it is, to help you stay accountable.

In the Results box, indicate the outcome of having created the goal from the dream.

Repeat the above steps for as long as you need to until you achieve your desired result(s). After that, move to the next habit you wish to remove and follow the same steps. Make your own SMART System Trackers to use on as many dreams/goals as you wish your child(ren) to realize.

As mentioned previously, the "Tools for Success" section in the back of this book provides additional SMART System Trackers, as well as various types of exercises for you and your children to use in order to integrate each of the 7 principles into your daily lives—and to live in faith and be as happy and successful as God intends. I hope you will turn to these exercises time and time again for inspiration, encouragement, and reinforcement of the ideals and values I know we share as Christians and parents.

Now, with the tips and tools we've explored so far, let's begin our journey together toward faith-based parenting and raising happy, successful children in today's challenging world.

Chapter 1

Show me your ways, Lord,
teach me your paths.

Guide me in your truth and teach me,
for you are God my Savior,
and my hope is in you all day long.

—Psalm 25:4–5 NIV

Principle #1

Seek the truth, and base your life on it.

Whatever else we may discover in life, nothing is more important than truth. Faith, trust, hope, and love are all based on truth, as is every other thing in life that is essential and meaningful. This is why I say to *seek the truth and base your life on it* is the first and most important thing to do. The first and most important thing that we all must do. It is principle number 1.

Toi and I have always told our daughters that at the end of the day, truth reigns. The truth is what we can stand on, day in and day out. Our family has always stressed how important it is to be truthful to ourselves, to each other, and to our God. That is the truth referred to in this principle. That is the truth we must seek and base our lives upon.

Seeking the truth in this way is not a simple matter. In fact, seeking the truth in this way will challenge your inner core. This truth will demand that you determine who you are and where you came from, and also what you are, who made you, and what you are made of. By forcing you to ask yourself where you came from and who you really are, the truth will ultimately lead you to wherever you go. I should qualify that by saying that not just any truth will lead you there; only God's truth can be your guide on the journey of life. This is why the words of the scripture that open this chapter are so important to always keep in mind: "Show me your ways, Lord, teach me your paths. Guide me in your truth and teach me, for you are God my Savior, and my hope is in you all day long" (Psalm 25:4–5 NIV).

Truth. Hope. Both are so essential. Dreams and goals are as well. They all shape our journey to a great extent, but one way or another, we each get to where we wind up. We create the path we travel by means of the choices we make. That's why I emphasized the importance of SMART dreams and goals in the introduction: because the way we get there is up to each of us. Truth, hope, and good choices and goals get us "there" successfully. Without these essentials, we just end up where we end up, usually feeling clueless, helpless, and hopeless. Faith—which is the spirit behind every attainable goal—is what makes success happen. But faith cannot happen without seeking the truth, without living it every day.

Below is another real-life example to illustrate this point.

Truth and Faith: The Magic of 7

For several years (it was actually 7—yes, that "magic" number yet again!), I worked with a beautiful human being named Linda. At the time, I was the campus president for a vocational college of five hundred students, and Linda was the top enrollment representative for all eight campuses in our family of schools. During that time, Linda also struggled with keeping her own daughter on the straight and narrow. A woman of tremendous faith, Linda often shared with me what her daughter was going through, telling me how Linda prayed she would turn her life around. After Linda and I had worked together for a few years, her daughter became pregnant. Although the upcoming birth of a child is always great news, Linda found her joy mixed with worry. She worried that having a baby in and of itself would not be enough to turn her daughter's life around.

"I just don't have a good feeling, La Shawn. What if the baby isn't enough to turn her life around?" Linda asked.

"Have faith, Linda."

"You know I have faith, but what if it isn't enough?"

"It's enough."

I felt it would be not just enough but everything. The Lord works in mysterious ways, and the only key to understanding those ways is faith. My own faith told me time would prove that I was right.

Sure enough, not long after sharing the great news that she would soon be a grandmother, Linda told me her daughter was going to come in and take a look at the programs we offered. "La Shawn, she's actually thinking about enrolling!" Linda said, her eyes and smile filled with love, hope, joy—and, most of all, faith.

I smiled back. "That's great, Linda. I have faith it's all going to work out just fine."

Linda looked at me, and we both burst out laughing.

I knew her faith was as strong as ever. Maybe even stronger.

As faith would have it, Linda's daughter did enroll in a program, and she obtained her AS degree in criminal justice. She continued her education, eventually getting her BA degree. Today she is a devoted mother and a respected professional, and she continues to remain on the straight and narrow road.

Linda's daughter's life completely changed, and I frequently reminded Linda that it was *her* faith that kept her daughter from falling even further, and it was *her* love and prayers that brought her daughter through.

As time went on, I often told Linda that although she might have thought her purpose at our college was to be the top enroller, to be rewarded with a generous salary and numerous accolades, perhaps that wasn't really her true purpose at all. Her true purpose might have been to share the stories about the many young lives she had positively impacted daily during her years at the college, all to provide examples that would encourage and inspire her daughter. In the end, perhaps it had all been so that her daughter would have a place waiting for her when she decided to change her life. It had never been about anything else, but because Linda was doing God's work for her daughter, a lot of other people benefited from Linda's efforts.

We never know how God will use our circumstances to change other people for the better. All we have to do is just stay faithful, walking in his light, for that is how we find the truth we seek—and that is also how we live in that truth.

The scripture we discussed earlier bears repeating: "Show me your ways, LORD, teach me your paths. Guide me in your truth and teach me, for you are God my Savior, and my hope is in you all day long" (Psalm 25:4–5 NIV).

So we can clearly see how great a role faith plays in principle number 1: *seek the truth, and base your life on it.* Seeking truth is a process, and living in truth is a process. Life itself is a process. Like any process, these endeavors require each of us to evaluate and then reevaluate the things that we currently base our lives on. Perhaps it's better to think of all this as a two-step process: first, seeking the truth, and second, living it, based on the evaluations entailed by the discoveries made during the seeking.

Fear: The Biggest Obstacle to Faith and Truth

Make no mistake: this is not an easy process. It's hard and often downright terrifying. Fear is the biggest reason why most people do not seek the truth. We all have a little of this fear in us, and so we must work hard to acknowledge that fear, and then work even harder to overcome it. That is our mission as human beings, as children of God, and, most important of all, as parents. God has entrusted each of us with the most sacred job on earth: being good moms and dads to our kids. We can't do it without seeking the truth and then living our lives based on the truth that we discover—not the truth we hoped to find, but the truth we do find, in all its raw, unvarnished reality.

When I think about seeking the truth, I think about having a clear path to where I want to go so that I am aware of everything that is true for me, as opposed to everything that is not true for me. That is what living in reality means.

Having a dream of what the future looks like helps steer us in the direction of truth. Knowing the truth and committing to live by it helps us create attainable goals that will make that dream reality. (Truth is a big part of SMART! And so is the absence of fear.)

In the words of Henry David Thoreau, "Go confidently in the direction of your dreams! Live the life you've imagined." To me, that quote means that in order to live a life that is both truthful and all that you want it to be, you have to first imagine it—you have to dream it before you can make it real.

Several years ago I got reconnected with how powerful dreams can be when I attended a dream conference in Chicago. We discussed Matthew Kelly's book *Dream Manager*, which describes how a company's dreams for its employees transformed not only the company but the individual employees. The book focuses on the inherent power within each of us to do great things, and that power stems from our ability to dream. The ability to dream is a uniquely human gift.

We also discussed several historical figures who overcame major life obstacles to make their dreams come true. These dreams were life-changing things that helped them each live a life based on truth. Abraham Lincoln, whose truth was based on the fact that although he was a product of his time, he knew slavery was wrong. Dr. Martin Luther King Jr., who dedicated his life to making his dream a reality, and who consequently lost his life because he sought to convey the truth that all men are created equal.

Life is full of heroes, small and large, who seek the truth and live by it. They follow principle number 1 and the wisdom of Psalm 25:4–5 whether they realize it or not. We learn about some of them and might be lucky enough to know some of them. As parents, we can each be heroes to our children by fearlessly seeking the truth, and modeling it for them by living lives based on the truth that we teach them. That is what Toi and I taught our daughters, and I credit that life's principle as a big contributing factor to the three of them being well-adjusted, successful young women today.

Remember, where faith is strong, fear cannot reign. Remember too that this is a big part of principle number 1: seek the truth, and base your life on it. Walk in God's light and truth every day, asking for his help and grace whenever you need to.

Now, let's move on to the next pages, where we'll put principle number 1 into practice.

Principle #1 in Practice

Seek the truth, and base your life on it.

Think about the situations in your life that have challenged a foundation of truth you were taught.

Write down what they were:

_____

_____

_____

_____

How did they affect you?

_____

_____

_____

_____

What changes did they cause you to make in your life?

_____

_____

_____

_____

How have they changed or affected you?

_____

_____

_____

What does principle number 1—*seek the truth, and base your life on it*—mean to you?

_____

_____

_____

What does the scripture verse we explored in this chapter mean to you? "Show me your ways, LORD, teach me your paths. Guide me in your truth and teach me, for you are God my Savior, and my hope is in you all day long" (Psalm 25:4–5 NIV).

_____

_____

_____

Now, have your child(ren) answer the above questions in an age-appropriate manner, following the SMART system described in the introduction (and then reinforced in chapters 5 and 6), which will help make their experiences that much more meaningful.

You can use the next pages as worksheets to help you guide your child(ren) to learn and practice age-appropriate, faith-based behavior and living.

Helping Your Children Put Principle #1 in Practice

Seek the truth, and base your life on it.

How do we seek the truth and then live our lives based on it? That's a pretty big job, so let's start by talking about things that have happened that have made you wonder about what was and wasn't true.

We can just talk about them, or you can write them down here:

_____

_____

_____

_____

How did you feel about this? Did it make you feel scared, mad, ashamed, or any other feeling?

_____

_____

_____

_____

What things should we change because of this? Can we change them? Why or why not?

_____

_____

_____

_____

What has happened because of these changes, or because of no changes?

_____

_____

_____

_____

Now that we've talked about it some more, what do you think it means to seek the truth, and base your life on it? Let's talk about it, and you can also write down how you feel about it, if you want to:

_____

_____

_____

Let's also talk about a scripture verse: "Show me your ways, LORD, teach me your paths. Guide me in your truth and teach me, for you are God my Savior, and my hope is in you all day long" (Psalm 25:4–5 NIV).

What do those words mean to you? How can we help God to teach us better and guide us better to live in truth? We can talk about this, and you can also write down your thoughts and feelings, if you want to:

_____

_____

_____

_____

Now that we have examined why it is essential to seek the truth and base our lives on it—and discussed practical ways to do so, and to teach our kids to do so as well—let's turn our attention to the next principle.

In the chapter that follows, we will explore principle number 2: _understand who you are by knowing your family history and traditions._

Chapter 2

For the promise is unto you, and to your children, and to all that are afar off, [even] as many as the LORD our God shall call.

—Acts 2:39 KJV

Principle #2

Understand who you are by knowing your family history and traditions.

Seeking the truth and basing your life on it is certainly essential to effective, faith-based living, but it is only the first step. In order to really live your truth, you have to know who you are, and the best way to do that is to understand where you come from.

You might be thinking, *I already know where I come from.* If you do, that's great. It will then be much easier for you to live in faith and to succeed in all your endeavors.

The thing is though, sometimes we think we know where we come from, but we don't really understand the full significance of our origins. Or we might discover the deepest truth lying in our core being, and it might be in conflict with our family of origin. That's why finding and living our truth must come first, and then we can adjust the rest as needed—if any adjustment is needed, that is.

Regardless, it is true for all of us that we need to know who we are (*seek and live our truth*) and we also need to know where we come from (*understand our origins*). That is the core message of principle number 2: *understand who you are by knowing your family history and traditions.*

As soon as they each were old enough to understand, Toi and I made family history and traditions an important part of our girls' experience. Experiences with family comprise some of the happiest memories of growing up—or at least they should. Such loving moments are key to a successful childhood and adolescence.

We told Talita, Tamani, and Tylyn, "You girls have a history that is rich and full of stories, even if we can't go back as far as some of your friends."

The girls grew up respecting that because we modeled it for them. In fact, perhaps it was just as important, if not even more so, that Toi and I also created our own traditions with our daughters. We did this throughout their growing-up years, and we still do it now that they are adults.

Let me share an example of one our newest family traditions.

Staying Connected Is a Family Affair

For the last couple of years, we have made it our mission to stay connected on a daily basis. This now includes not just Toi and me and our three daughters, but also my son-in-law (Talita's husband, Paul). As our immediate family expands, the tradition will extend to all our new family members.

We are each assigned a day in which we are responsible for sending out a message via text or e-mail to the other members of the family. This can be a word, a phrase, a famous quotation—anything that will inspire or lift the rest of us up. This is a great tradition not just because it keeps us connected but because it inevitably seems to come at the right time; if not for all of us, then at least for one of us, usually the one who happens to be struggling a little bit on that particular day.

These are hectic, stressful times. Pretty much every day brings a challenge of one sort or another. This is true for everyone, not just my family and me. Words of encouragement and inspiration from a loved one can mean so much at any time, but especially during a difficult time or in the midst of a moment fraught with tension.

Maybe a new tradition like the one my family developed could make all the difference to your family, especially your child(ren). Don't assume that SnapChat, Instagram, Twitter, Tumblr, Facebook, or the coolest new app can take the place of the best life has to offer young people: a loving parent and a loving God, through whom all other love and blessings flow. Text a message of love and inspiration to your child right now, and see how he or she responds.

Know Yourself

Whether you follow classic family traditions, invent new ones, or use a combination as Toi and I do, family history and traditions are invaluable. They center and ground us. They show us that we belong. They teach us how to trust. In addition, they help us learn how to reach out, and at the same time, how to go within … how to understand ourselves by knowing who we are.

Remember, in order to truly become the best version of yourself, you must know yourself; in order to know yourself, you must know where you come from. When I say "know yourself" in this sense, I mean *really* know yourself, not just the reflection in the mirror, not just the house and car, or the money in the bank, or the diploma on the wall, or any of those things. I'm talking about the real you, the core known to only you and God and maybe one other person (or two or three other people).

Know who you are, what your truth is, what you live for. It starts with truth, and it's reinforced by family and traditions. You understand who you are by how you fit—or don't, and might not even want to.

Once again we can see the importance of principle number 2: *understand who you are by knowing your family history and traditions.* Learn about your culture, study your history, and discover your family traditions. This is how you find yourself. This is how you find and live your truth without getting lost or sidetracked by things that aren't part of your core, or by people who don't have your best interest at heart.

Another way of putting this is saying that you can achieve a healthy life only by first having a healthy self. That process includes a study of where you came from. So, by understanding your own culture, your family history and traditions, you will learn to appreciate who you are, and then you will be able to teach others about yourself, your family, your ancestors, and your culture.

Achieving this allows us to increase the understanding of those around us. This is the point where we model behavior that encourages others to cast off stereotypes and renounce prejudices. These exist in all of us, and it's up to all of us to release them. One at a time, person by person, this is exactly what we need to do. Individually and together, we need to let the walls of misunderstanding fall down all around us, and then the gates of understanding will open up before us. This is the way to true happiness—the only way—but it has to start with having a true understanding of ourselves, which will lead us to a deeper understanding of our fellow humans.

This is what life is really about; this is what God wants us to do for ourselves and for one another. Just as the scripture that opens this chapter states: "For the promise is unto you, and to your children, and to all that are afar off, [even] as many as the LORD our God shall call" (Acts 2:39 KJV).

Understanding, Acceptance, and Love

The lessons of understanding are infinite, just like the lessons of love and faith. Although it is key to understand yourself, it is also important to understand others, as described above, because this is what both enriches life and helps heal the world. This kind of understanding is deep, it comes from the heart as well as the mind; it leads to one of the pearls of faith and presence, *acceptance*.

True acceptance comes from first understanding and loving yourself, and then understanding and loving other people. And it all begins with practicing principle number 2: *understand who you are by knowing your family history and traditions*. This history and system of traditions includes the greater culture of which your individual family is a part.

We can now see that embracing the principles described in this book will help us achieve a deeper and more lasting sense of self not only for ourselves but also for our fellow humans, our brothers and sisters in the greater sense. This allows us more happiness in a much deeper way. I'm talking about the true happiness that comes from within, from the depths of the individual soul, and also from all those around us, which comprise the collective soul of humanity—God's eternal love moving through each of us and all of us.

It may take a lifetime to achieve this, but it is worth the effort. Well worth it. And the process of getting there is what life is really about. It's the journey God wants us to take, and the path he wants us to travel. Yet again, this chapter's scripture verse speaks to reinforce this for us: "For the promise is unto you, and to your children, and to all that are afar off, [even] as many as the LORD our God shall call" (Acts 2:39 KJV).

The Wealth of History—The Value of Tradition

As I've shared, Toi and I do not have a great deal of financial wealth from our history to share with our girls, but we do have a wealth of history. We have shared that with them over the years, and we continue to do so. Now we look forward to sharing that wealth of history and heritage with our grandchildren, and to watching our daughters share with their own children what we shared with them throughout their growing-up years.

This wealth of history includes many stories about our ancestors, as well as photographs of people from past generations. There is nothing like coming across a photo that bears an image of a person who looks just like you! Many times one of the girls would excitedly say, "Wow, Dad, I look like her!" Or, "Hey, Mom, this old guy has eyes just like mine!"

Looking through family photos and sharing family stories is a great way to honor older traditions and also to create new ones. This experience was valuable and rewarding for Talita, Tamani, and Tylyn. It validated for them that they have history, that our family has a story, and that our story connects them to something bigger than themselves. In particular, it showed them that our family history and traditions are just as valuable and special as those of other families originating from Europe or Asia or any of the various parts of the world.

In other words, building self-worth develops from understanding yourself, your family history and traditions, and your culture. Once you understand this, you can understand others and their history, traditions, and culture. As we've discussed, this understanding leads to acceptance. It also leads to respect. This is what will teach our children to be better people and to create a better world.

All that said, we must remember that families don't operate in a vacuum, and children can't grow up in one, either. This is just part of life. Faith is a gift but also a test. Understanding your family history entails realizing and accepting that families have issues—your family, my family, every family.

Let me share another real-life example.

Home Is Where the Heart—And Laughter—Is

When I was growing up, we spent every holiday at my grandmother's house. I can still vividly recall these events. The family would gather to eat, laugh, and tell stories, some of which we would make up as we went along. This was a rich tradition for me to draw on. And it was incredibly fun. There was no limit to the laughter. Whether it was my uncle reading palms and making crazy predictions, or my auntie asking ridiculously personal questions, this was the only "normal" I knew. It was our family tradition, although I didn't term it that until much later.

During my growing-up years, I thought all families—all Black families, I should say—operated this way. But as I got older, I would ask myself if this was how I would interact with my own immediate family one day. The more I thought about it, the more I realized it just wasn't how I wanted to be. It wasn't the family life I wanted to create for my future wife and the children we would have. Don't get me wrong: my family of origin was entertaining and downright funny; to this very day, I smile thinking about some of the laughs we had as a family at Grandma's house.

Laughter is important, but it isn't strong enough to create the foundation needed for a family. When I realized this, it made me think a lot about my family, history, traditions, and culture. It made me question how I would want my children to remember our family. What would their childhood memories be like? I thought about this long and hard.

In the end, this was one of the main reasons behind our move to Northern California. At age thirty-three, I took my wife and daughters, and we relocated to a place where we had no family or friends, and I must admit, for the sake of my family history and traditions, it was the best thing I have ever done. I love my extended family, I love my family of origin, and I appreciate the rich history it has given me. But I also recognize that understanding who we are and where we come from is something we each have to examine on a deeper level. By that I mean if we see that our family history and traditions might directly affect our future in a way other than what we desire, we have to move away from it. We have to achieve the distance that will allow us to create some new history and our own new path.

In other words, another way to think about principle number 2 —*understand who you are by knowing your family history and traditions*—is to recognize that although we are all products of our history and culture, and we must understand and accept that, we must also know that we are not locked in by it; in fact, we have the power to move beyond our history. It is part of who we are, but it is not all we are.

I accept my history, and I am proud of it. One of the things about my own history that I am proudest of is my name. Out of more than seventy-five first cousins (yes, there is that magic number 7, yet again!), I am the only grandchild my paternal grandmother named. I must admit it took me many years to understand just how special the name La Shawn Bouvier Wells really is, but once I came to understand the facts around my name, it meant the world to me. To this day, whenever I say my name, I do so with great pride, smiling and knowing I am a living memory of Katie Wells[MJO3] [LSW4].

Another part of my history essential to who I am is my faith. I deeply appreciate and honor my mother, Troy Wells, who was instrumental in instilling my faith at an early age. My name is important to me, but my faith and soul are even more so.

Whether you focus on your name, your origins, your history, your traditions, or your culture, the point is to know the real you. Understand who you are by knowing your family history and traditions. You'll never truly succeed in life unless and until you do.

That said, let's move on to the next pages, where we will put principle number 2 into practice.

Principle #2 in Practice

Understand who you are by knowing your family history and traditions.

To see where your place is in your family, do a family tree. You can use the template below:

<u>Family Tree</u>

_____ & _____   _____ & _____

↓ ⋁

_____ & _____   _____ & _____

_____ & _____

⟍ ↙ ↓

....

↓

_____

To give you an idea of how it should look once it's filled in, here's my family tree:

<u>Family Tree</u>

Albert & Troy   John & Amina

Yolanda & La Shawn   Toi

La Shawn & Toi

⟍ ↙ ↓

↓Talita & Paul Tamani   Tylyn

London

Write down how you feel about your place in the family. How did being the eldest/youngest/middle/etc., affect you?

_____

_____

_____

_____

List the people from your family of origin (and/or from your extended family) who touched your life. Find a way to personally thank each of them. (Remember, those who have passed on you can still thank through prayer.)

_____

_____

_____

_____

Create a tradition for you and your immediate family, and then share it with your existing community.

_____

_____

_____

_____

Creating new traditions can be a bit intimidating. To get you started, here are a few family traditions Toi and I have created:

- During the holiday season, we put the names of all our immediate family members into a hat. We each pick a name, and then we cannot buy a gift for that particular person; we have to make a gift, trade something of value with that person, or agree to do a service for him or her, with a start and finish time attached to it.
- On Christmas Eve, we read "A Visit from Saint Nicholas," "Three Trees," and the story of the birth of Jesus from the Bible.
- I cook jambalaya every New Year's Day.
- Each family member has made a dream book.

What does principle number 2—*understand who you are by knowing your family history and traditions*—mean to you?

_____

_____

_____

_____

What does the scripture verse we explored in this chapter mean to you? "For the promise is unto you, and to your children, and to all that are afar off, [even] as many as the LORD our God shall call" (Acts 2:39 KJV).

_____

_____

_____

_____

Now, have your child(ren) answer the above questions in an age-appropriate manner, following the SMART system described in the introduction (and then reinforced in chapters 5 and 6), which will help make their experiences that much more meaningful.

You can use the next pages as worksheets to help you guide your child(ren) to learn and practice age-appropriate, faith-based behavior and living.

Helping Your Children Put Principle #2 in Practice

Understand who you are by knowing your family history and traditions.

Let's make a family tree!

Family Tree

_____ & _____   _____ & _____

_____ & _____   _____ & _____

_____ & _____

_____   _____   _____

_____

How do you feel about being the oldest/middle/youngest/etc.? We can just talk about this, or you can write down your feelings here:

_____

_____

_____

_____

Who in our family has really made a big difference in your life? It's okay—you don't have to say Mom or Dad!

_____

_____

_____

_____

Let's think of a special way to thank _____ (fill in the name[s] of those listed above).

_____

_____

_____

What traditions do we have as a family that you like or don't like?

_____

_____

_____

Let's make some new traditions! We can even share them with our friends and people we know in the community:

_____

_____

_____

We've talked about it a bit, so what do you think it means to understand who you are by knowing your family history and traditions? Let's talk about it, and you can also write down how you feel about it, if you want to:

_____

_____

_____

Let's also talk about a scripture verse: "For the promise is unto you, and to your children, and to all that are afar off, [even] as many as the LORD our God shall call" (Acts 2:39 KJV).

What do those words mean to you? How can we keep this promise to God? We can talk about this, and you can also write down your thoughts and feelings, if you want to:

_____

_____

_____

Now that we have examined why it is so important to understand who we are by knowing our family history and traditions—and discussed practical ways to do so, and to teach our kids to do so as well—let's turn our attention to the next principle.

In the chapter that follows, we will explore principle number 3: *be family oriented.*

Chapter 3

Children are a gift from the LORD;
they are a reward from him.

Children born to a young man
are like arrows in a warrior's hands.

How joyful is the man whose quiver is full of them!
He will not be put to shame when he confronts his accusers at the city gates.

—Psalm 127:3–5 NLT

Principle #3

Be family oriented.

Once you base your life on your truth, once you know who you are because you understand where you come from, the next logical step is to share that wisdom and faith with those closest to you: your family. That brings us from principle number 1 (*seek the truth and base your life on it*) and principle number 2 (*understand who you are by knowing your family history and traditions*) to principle number 3: *be family oriented.* Throughout this chapter, we'll explore how and why family plays such an important role in faith-based living—and, of course, faith-based parenting.

Before we go any further, let's understand that *family* can be biological, social, or a combination of the two. In this sense, "family" simply means those people who love and care about us and whom we love and care about. We each need people to love, and we each also need people who love us. We each also need people we can trust and rely on, no matter what. Those people, in turn, know that they can trust and rely on us, no matter what. The no-matter-what aspect is what makes us family to one another. Sometimes that develops from blood ties; sometimes it develops from a shared experience or a common belief; sometimes it evolves as a result of just "clicking" with another person. Whichever way it happens, it is an unshakable, irrefutable bond that we rely on—*no matter what.*

The essence of being family oriented is the assurance of knowing there is a core group of people whom you love, trust, and can rely on—and who feel the same way about you—yes, to repeat, no matter what! That's what family is, and that's what family does. If you don't have that with your family of origin, or with your current immediate or extended family, it's essential to seek it socially, whether in church, or with another faith-based group, or in a community organization that provides true nurturing and valuable support.

It is true that people who have love in their lives from early childhood onward are usually better able to receive love and to give love to others, but anyone can learn how to give and receive love. The only requirement is to want to love and be loved. That's it!

So today is the day to start being family oriented—both with your own family (if you are blessed to have one), your church, your community, and your world. Doing this means that all children—who, as the adults of tomorrow, are the world's future—will enjoy a solid upbringing, regardless of whether both parents are physically present in their lives.

Understand that in no way am I minimizing the wonder and blessing of two-parent households. Mother and father, together, create a sense of family like no other. Toi and I have built our life around that. But for a variety of reasons—many of them often beyond our control—that wonder and blessing do not always occur in every family. That doesn't mean we can't all be family oriented. We can, and we must, be family oriented.

In this context, being family oriented means embodying the creed: "It takes a village to raise a child." Now sometimes that "village" might be extended family; other times it might be a larger external community, a village in the literal sense. It is always a group that cares, that loves, that values the child as both an individual *and* a future adult, the combination of innocence that must be protected and potential that must be nurtured. This is essential to faith-based parenting.

To further illustrate what I mean, let me share a real-life example.

It Might Take a Village, but It Starts at Home

I can speak from experience when I say we must be family oriented, whether that family is biological, social, or a combination of the two. It is not just a principle I recommend, it is an absolute necessity. Having faith entails being part of a family.

I've already shared some of my experiences with my extended family, from adulthood and my growing-up years. But I haven't yet shared my experiences related to my immediate family of origin. That's because my family life changed abruptly during my childhood.

My mother and father divorced when I was seven years old. (There is that number 7 again.) As a result, I was prematurely thrust into manhood. This is not an exaggeration.

On that fateful day, my father led me to the front door, bent down, and looked me squarely in the eyes. "La Shawn, you are now the man of the house. Take care of your mother and sister." He walked out then, closing the door.

I just stood there, too stunned to even go to the window to watch him leave. The car engine turned over, and he was gone. It began and ended that suddenly. No discussion, no options, no anything. Our two-parent family was over, and that was that.

My point in relating this is that my father's statement to me, along with the breakup of my parents' marriage, could have destroyed my soul. But it didn't. And the reason why it didn't was that my mother, my biological extended family, and my social community were still there. They set up a rock-solid support system that sustained me short- and long-term. My mother and all the adults around me were *family oriented*. Together they provided the home—and the village—that it took to raise me, bringing me from childhood to adulthood on a foundation of love and faith. They understood and appreciated the scripture verse that opens this chapter (Psalm 127:3 NLT), especially the fact that "Children are a gift from the Lord; they are a reward from him."

Why Family Is the Foundation of Faith

Whether biological, social, or a combination of the two, family is the foundation of faith. You may not have had the blessing of a strong, loving family. You may not live in a faith-based community. Family may not be something that you had, but it is always something that you can build.

You can't change the past; no one can. But you can change the present, and you can do what you need to do in order to ensure that the future will be as close as possible to what you hope it will be. We can all do that, and we all must do that. This is all part of what it means to be family oriented. It is also part of recognizing not just that "Children are a gift from the Lord; they are a reward from him" (Psalm 127:3 NLT), as the scripture tells us, but also that we, as parents and adults, are responsible for children, the adults of tomorrow. I shared the example from my own childhood to illustrate exactly that, because every adult in my "village" wasn't a parent—certainly they all weren't *my* parents … the only biological parent who was there for me throughout my childhood was my mother. But they all taught me what it meant to *be family oriented.*

Yes, family is the foundation of faith; however, that doesn't mean that our first encounter with faith happens with our family origin. It just so happens that mine did. To a great extent, I lived and practiced principle number 3 before any of the others, but not everyone can be so lucky. Your experience might have been similar to mine, vastly different, or somewhere in between. The point is, the family of origin is not the starting point of faith for everyone, and that is why I have made it principle number 3 (not 1 or 2). I recommend that you follow that order as well; otherwise, feeling that you missed out on the kind of family of origin that you hoped for, or wished you might have had, could cause you to give up on practicing all the other principles altogether. Too many people blame all their failures on the family they had—or didn't have—instead of simply accepting responsibility and starting tomorrow today. That is, living a life based on truth, integrity, accountability, and faith. Conversely, having a wonderful, loving, faith-filled family might make s person complacent and liable to feel no further work on faith is necessary. Of course, this is never true: we can always learn and grow and build. This is also part of what it means to *be family oriented.*

Mom, Dad, or Village—Today's Children Need *You*

The example I've shared from my own childhood illustrates why it is so important to be family oriented, not just for your own family (that is, your biological one) but for other families too, and for all those people who don't have a family at all—particularly for children who have no family, no adult to guide them or to model faith-based living for them. Do you know anyone who fits this description? Do you know a child (or an adult) who is in need of someone to model faith-based living, or just to extend a hand in friendship, or to offer a heart filled with caring? It could be a person who is biologically or socially related to you. But whomever it is, that person is someone in need of family *and* faith. That person is waiting for you. And be aware that adults who lacked family support during their biological (or chronological) childhoods remain "children" in the emotional sense. Just as God is the Father to all of us, so must we be "parents" to all "children" in need—at least in terms of modeling faith-based behavior. If you're raising an eyebrow right now, remember that reaching out in this way to your brother or sister in need might make him or her a better parent to an actual child in the present or future. It's not for us to judge, just to love and help. That's another aspect of being part of the "village."

Thus, in order to continue to move toward that blissful, dreamed-of existence aspired to by people of faith, you must practice principle number 3: *be family oriented* (whether biologically, socially, or in combination).

It does take moms, dads (or both together, if possible), communities ("villages"), and God. And it takes *you*—each and every one of us, whether we are biological parents or not.

Remember the scripture verse opening this chapter:

Children are a gift from the LORD;
they are a reward from him.

Children born to a young man
are like arrows in a warrior's hands.

How joyful is the man whose quiver is full of them!
He will not be put to shame when he confronts his accusers at the city gates.

—Psalm 127:3–5 NLT

The first verse is the most essential for our purposes, because gifts and rewards, though miraculous and wonderful, do entail responsibilities. We may be blessed, but that doesn't mean we don't have to do the work that is part and parcel of the blessing. The harvest of a garden, orchard, or farm is a blessing, but it cannot be reaped without work, without cultivation. Children and family are much the same: a combination of blessing and cultivation, just like all faith-based living.

Work with your own family to achieve the love that families should have. But also reach out to those who don't have a family or who need assistance with the family that they do have. Provide them with love, caring, teaching, understanding, patience, presence, empathy, and whatever else they need. Model faith-based behavior, and teach your child(ren) to do the same. By doing this, we create happiness not only for ourselves but also for those around us. The more people in our communities that feel loved and cared for, the more likely that love will spread—both within individual communities and outward to the larger world. The more children, teens, and adults there are who are happy in our communities, the greater each and all of our chances will be to experience true and lasting happiness. Faith is always the answer, and a key part of that is always to *be family oriented* (whether biological, social, or a combination of the two).

When It Comes to *Your* Family, Just Be There!

For those of us blessed with a biological family—whether or not we are biological parents—that family should always come first. There's no other way to say it, so please forgive me if it sounds blunt. Nothing should ever come before your family.

Let me use another example from my own life to explain what I mean. This time it's something related to my wife and children, not my own childhood and family of origin.

I've already described that all three of our daughters were student athletes. Given what I've shared about Toi's and my commitment to parenting, you won't be surprised to learn that we never missed a single one of our three daughters' meets or games. However, in addition, no matter which of the three had an event, her two sisters were always there as well.

Other people at the meets or games would often turn to Toi or me, exclaiming, "Wow! Your other kids came too!" The tone of voice and facial expression always indicated that this was a shock for them.

Talita, Tamani, and Tylyn were always equally shocked! Whichever two sat in the stands with Toi and me, watching their sister play or run, would look at us as if to say, "Mom, Dad, what is *wrong* with these people?"

Toi and I would just smile at each other because that was exactly the way we wanted our daughters to respond to the onlookers' shock.

For us, when it comes to family, just be there. That's how it was when the girls were growing up, and, to a great extent, it's how it still is and always will be. It was something that we instilled in and expected from our girls early on. We still do, though, of course, we've adjusted this expectation accordingly as they grew through adolescence and into adulthood. Such expectations must always be flexible as children become teens and then adults.

To think of this another way, the outward display of this may change as children grow older, but the inward feeling does not change—and it never will. This is just an inherent aspect of principle number 3: *be family oriented*. And so, if someone in your family, someone you love and who loves you, is doing something that is important to him or her, it is your responsibility to make it a priority and to be there.

As a parent modeling the principle of being family oriented, it is your responsibility to create the guidelines for how the family should interact. Toi and I always created these kinds of guidelines, and we insisted that our girls follow them. They knew what we expected, and because we always did what we expected them to do, they appreciated and valued the behavior modeled. Our daughters supported one another because we supported each other and each of them. It was never "I have to go to my sister's game/meet; my parents make me"; it was always "My sisters and I always go to one another's games and meets. Our parents always come too. It's so great!"

I don't say all this because I'm their dad and want to believe it's true. I say it because I have witnessed it time and again. For the past twenty years, I have had the privilege of coaching girls' softball. My daughters have become involved in that effort, making themselves part of the community and paying forward what they received from their mom and me, and also from their respective teams when they were growing up.

As of this writing, only the eldest, Talita, is a parent in her own right. But Talita, Tamani, and Tylyn all understand what it means to practice principle number 3: *be family oriented*. They understand that we each make up the "village" required to raise a child, and that we each are responsible for the "gift" and "reward" that every single child is to us through God's grace (as described in Psalm 127:3–5 NLT).

Family—For Better *and* for Worse

Family dynamics change quite frequently during the course of our lives. Sometimes these changes are for the better, and sometimes they are for the worse—or even for the worst—nevertheless, we can and should expect they will change.

Here is another illustration from my own extended family, this time from adulthood. When my maternal grandmother passed, I saw what it did to our entire family. We went from being a group who met for every holiday to one that hardly saw or spoke to one another. Whereas once we had gathered at my grandmother's house to share stories, laughter, food, and, most of all, love, after she was gone, we became like strangers—worse yet, enemies. We had been the closest group of people on earth. Or at least it seemed that way to me as a child and teenager. With her passing, we turned into a group that fell out over money, and I am talking about a small amount of dollars in the grand scheme of things. My aunts and uncles (brothers and sisters to one another) made crazy accusations as to whom took what, and some of them even stopped speaking to each other for years.

I sought to stay out of it, but I was dragged into the whole mess when one of my uncles, whom I had been extremely close with up to that point, accused my mother of conspiring with one of my aunts to steal my grandmother's house. In fact, my grandmother had left the house to my aunt, with specific instructions that she was to do whatever she wanted with it. No amount of explaining, patiently or otherwise, could get my uncle to believe this, much less accept it.

As sad as it was for me to have a rift with my favorite uncle, there was something sadder still that happened as a result of the whole situation. I had a falling out with one of my cousins, who was like a brother to me, because he wanted to get in the middle of the situation, even after I warned him that we grandkids should let our parents' generation figure things out. To make a long and very sad story short, he didn't heed my advice. From that very day until the day he passed (some six years later), our relationship was never the same. Sometimes the damage done to our bonds with those closest to us are irreparable. It was that case with my cousin and me, and, as a result, I lost one of the best friends I ever had—or ever will have—six years before he died. There was nothing I could do about the time we lost as a result of his passing; that was in God's hands. But the six years prior was in my hands, and in my cousin's hands, and we threw it away for nothing. Now there is no way to get those six years back. Ever. So before you let a rift develop, remember how much is at risk. Nothing is irreparable between family members. Where there is love, there is also forgiveness. Always …

That said, here is another example from my family of origin—this one is about how things with family can be not just for the better, but for the best. As with much of the best from my growing-up years, this story centers on my mother. She stepped up to raise my younger cousin after his own mom died when he was just two years old. His dad, my mom's brother, was serving his country in Vietnam. Because of my mother's selfless act, my cousin grew up with me in our house. He and I were like brothers. Even after his dad returned home, he continued to live with us. To this day, I love him like a brother. And I always will.

I am also glad to say that, even though it has taken almost ten years, for the most part, my family has recovered from the death of my grandmother. We've returned to having family gatherings, especially at holiday time, where we again share great stories, hysterical laughs, and fantastic food. It isn't the same without my grandmother or my cousin, of course, but we do the best we can. Just being there for each other is the best way to honor the memories of those we have lost.

We can each do this with our own families. And we should! We should also join groups to extend our families outward to the larger community. In this way, we can share love, faith, and all our blessings with as many people as possible. I have been blessed over the last twenty years to extend my family through my work as a girls' softball coach. This has provided me with the opportunity to meet some great families that I have included in my social family. I encourage you to become part of your community's family, which will only enrich your and your family's life with joy, friendship, and love. That is the essence of what it means to *be family oriented*—biologically, socially, and in combination.

Most of all, remember that your child(ren) will emulate the behaviors that they observe. If you want them to be family oriented, you have to model that behavior first. Do and be what you hope your child(ren) will do and be, and then smile as you watch it happen.

Having explored the importance of what it means to *be family oriented*, let's move on to the next pages, where we will put principle number 3 into practice.

Principle #3 in Practice

Be family oriented.

Remember the family tree from the last chapter? Fill it in again using the template below:

Family Tree

_____ & _____   _____ & _____

_____ & _____   _____ & _____

_____ & _____

_____ _____   _____

_____

Using your family tree (above), think about the biological family relationships that you have. Are they the way you would like them to be? Why or why not?

_____

_____

_____

_____

Describe some ways in which you can make these relationships better, or at least more in line with the way you would like them to be:

_____

_____

_____

Commit to some action steps to make the changes described above:

_____

_____

_____

Describe your social family:

_____

_____

_____

What are your community (social family) responsibilities? If you don't have any, how can you find a way to reach out to your community?

_____

_____

_____

Commit to some action steps to make the changes described above:

_____

_____

_____

Describe some of the ways in which you can improve or enhance your existing social relationships:

_____

_____

_____

Commit to some action steps to make the changes described above:

_____

_____

_____

What does principle number 3—*be family oriented*—mean to you?

_____

_____

_____

Think about the first line of the scripture verse opening this chapter:
"Children are a gift from the LORD; they are a reward from him" (Psalm 127:3
NLT). What does that mean to you?

_____

_____

_____

Now, have your child(ren) answer the above questions in an age-appropriate manner, following the SMART system described in the introduction (and then reinforced in chapters 5 and 6), which will help make their experiences that much more meaningful.

You can use the next pages as worksheets to help you guide your child(ren) to learn and practice age-appropriate, faith-based behavior and living.

Helping Your Children Put Principle #3 in Practice

Be family oriented.

Remember the family tree we did? Let's do another one!

Family Tree

_____ & _____   _____ & _____

_____ & _____   _____ & _____

_____ & _____

_____ _____ _____ _____

_____

Think about our family. Is everything the way you would like it to be? Why or why not? We can talk about this, or you can write down your feelings here:

_____

_____

_____

_____

How can we make any of these things better, or at least more like you wish they could be?

_____

_____

_____

_____

Let's do these things, and see if we can make the changes happen:

_____

_____

_____

Do you have any friends at school or on teams or in church who feel like family to you?

_____

_____

_____

What jobs do you have at home or at school or on your team or in church? If you don't have any, would you like some?

_____

_____

_____

Let's figure out how you can take on some jobs or add some new ones:

_____

_____

_____

Do you think you can be a better friend or teammate? Why or why not?

_____

_____

_____

If you want to be a better friend or teammate, let's figure out how you can do it:

_____

_____

_____

_____

Why is family important? Which is more important, our "real" family that we are related to or our friends who feel like family? Why? What is the difference between the two?

_____

_____

_____

_____

Let's also talk about a scripture verse (Psalm 127:3 NLT): "Children are a gift from the LORD; they are a reward from him."

What do those words mean to you? How do you think God wants us to use his gifts and rewards? We can talk about this, and you can also write down your thoughts and feelings, if you want to:

_____

_____

_____

_____

After our examination of why it is so important to be family oriented (whether that refers to biological or social "family" or a combination of the two)—and discussed practical ways to model this behavior, and to teach our kids to do so as well—let's turn our attention to the next principle.

In the chapter that follows, we will explore principle number 4: *be selective about your friends.*

Chapter 4

He that walketh with wise [men] shall be wise: but a companion of fools shall be destroyed.

—Proverb 13:20 KJV

Principle #4

Be selective about your friends.

We've examined the importance of living our truth, knowing who we are by understanding our family history and traditions, and being family oriented (principle numbers 1, 2, and 3, respectively). Furthermore, while discussing the importance of being family oriented (in the previous chapter), we saw how that can mean biological or social family, or a combination of the two. Our community is part of our social family, and so is our church. But for most of us, the most essential members of our social family are our friends. Many, many people feel their friends are more important than biological family. For youngsters—and adolescents, in particular—this is especially true.

I've already shared my belief that family takes priority. That doesn't mean I don't value friendship; I value it highly. I've described the cousin who was one of the best friends I ever had or ever will have. After reading the dedication at the beginning of this book, you know that my wife is also my best friend. I qualify "social" family because the lines blur between family and deep friendship, and between love and deep friendship. Sometimes they are very special relationships that can qualify as both; sometimes not. Emotions are powerful, and they can easily overwhelm intelligence, good judgment, and even our sense of right and wrong. We inherit our biological family, but we choose the people we fall in love with and the people we become friends with. It's critical to choose them wisely and well.

Here again, as parents, we must model that behavior for our child(ren). We can do so by practicing principle number 4: *be selective about your friends*. We will explore how to do exactly that throughout this chapter, as well as looking at why wisely and carefully choosing friends is such an important aspect of faith-based living—and, of course, faith-based parenting too. (Remember that kids emulate the behavior they observe, so if you want them to be selective about their friends, you have to be selective about your friends first.)

The Company We Keep

We all know the expression; we're judged by the company we keep. This is true because we choose our friends, as stated above. Whom we choose reflects our judgment, our integrity, our character, our likes and dislikes. Again, nurturing and lasting friendships depend on choosing wisely and well. This is the way to build relationships based on trust and reciprocity. We don't want to be involved with users or manipulators; we certainly don't want our children to be.

In essence, this is the gist of the scripture verse opening this chapter: "He that walketh with wise [men] shall be wise: but a companion of fools shall be destroyed" (Proverb 13:20 KJV). Choose wisely. Don't be deceived by fools (or users or manipulators or anyone immoral or evil or fill in the blank with your own worst fear as a parent).

All three of our daughters will tell you that Toi and I always told them, "Girls, choose your friends wisely." We inculcated this from the very beginning, as soon as they each were old enough to understand what we meant. As the eldest, Talita modeled this for Tamani, and then both of them modeled it for Tylyn, who is several years younger. They grew up watching their mother and me choose our own friends wisely, in addition to watching their sisters do the same by modeling our and one another's behavior. Did any of the girls ever have a friend whom Toi and I felt was less than ideal for a variety of reasons? Of course they did. Learning how to choose friends wisely is part of growing up; it's part of life. Even adults suffer the disappointment of being hurt and betrayed by so-called friends. Toi has. I have. You have. Everyone has. As I said, it's part of life.

Of course, it's being part of life doesn't make it hurt any less. Why can't we avoid the pain of it? Why can't we follow the advice in Proverb 13:20 more closely?

There are two deceptively simple answers to the above questions. The first answer is because we are human. The second answer is because pain is one of our greatest teachers (love and faith are the others, but they usually work more effectively after we've experienced the pain that wakes us up).

The answers are deceptively simple because the questions are extremely complicated. They might seem as simple as the answers, but, just like those answers, these questions are anything but simple.

Let's look at the question a little bit differently, adding some more depth to it so it doesn't seem so simple: Why does it take us so long to realize the person we are closest to may not be the best person for us? Is this something we learn as kids? Yes, that brings it into sharper focus. There aren't too many of us who can read that without squirming just a bit, even if only in recollection. You might be closest to the person who is 100 percent right for you—*now*. But was it always that way? Have you "lucked out" with your spouse and closest friends, or did you learn the hard way?

Think about some of your earliest friendships. No matter what type of friendships they were—"boyfriend/girlfriend" or strictly platonic—if they were positive relationships, you usually stayed out of trouble. By "positive," I mean mutually beneficial and nurturing. If they were not positive (that is, if they were the opposite of beneficial and nurturing), you likely got into trouble, sometimes just by association. You were judged by the company you kept, just as we all have been at one time or another.

What company do *you* keep? Who are the people in your closest circle of friends? Do they encourage you to learn and grow, or do they feel threatened if you attempt to do so? Do they help you achieve your goals, or do they sabotage your success (in overt or covert ways)?

No matter what other role he or she may play in your life, a true friend will always display certain behaviors: a true friend will help you face and conquer your fears; a true friend will cheer your successes and help you fulfill your dreams; a true friend will accept you as you are while encouraging and inspiring you to be and do the best you can; a true friend will always love and forgive you.

A friend who doesn't do these things is not a *true* friend. So be careful about the people you give the title of friend to in the first place. Remember and practice principle number 4: *be selective about your friends.* Don't be counted a companion of fools—or worse.

I'd like to share two examples of friendship: one the nurturing and beneficial kind, the other exactly the opposite. Although neither of these were friendships of mine or of any member of my family, they are real-life examples (one was a boy who attended our church, and the other was girl I coached in softball). Let's see what these two youngsters learned about the importance of choosing friends wisely and well.

A Tale of Two Friendships

Over the years of attending the same church, Toi and I and our girls became good friends with many wonderful people. One Sunday, we saw a new family in the midst of the familiar flock: mother, father, and teenage son. We made our way over to them to say hello after the service ended.

James and I introduced ourselves as we shook hands. Caroline and Toi did the same.

I engaged James in some small talk, discovering that he was a mechanic who owned his own shop. I filed this away for future reference, and we chatted amicably for a few minutes.

I heard Caroline tell Toi, "I don't work outside the home, and I sure hope I'll find some ways to do good work here at the church or in some other worthwhile place."

Toi smiled at her, catching my eye. My wife likes her relationships to have meaning, and she doesn't care much for superficial people or behavior. I'd hoped she'd found a new friend.

Meanwhile, Talita had taken the lead with James and Caroline's son, Luke. He looked about the same age as Tamani, and the two seemed to be sizing each other up shyly, as teens so often do. Talita dominated the conversation, and Tylyn stood quietly beside her oldest sister.

I watched all this while I continued to talk with James. Although Luke chatted with Talita, he was watching a girl a few yards away. We all knew this girl. Her name was Cecelia, and she was what I will call a "flirt." She was a little bit younger than Talita and a little bit older than Tamani; neither one liked her too much, which was fine with Toi and me. As Toi put it, "That girl is a piece of work. Nothing but trouble."

Knowing my daughters as I do, I was sure neither Talita nor Tamani would miss Luke's behavior.

Sure enough, while in the car driving home, Tamani said, "Luke might've been talking to you, but he sure wasn't looking at you."

Talita laughed. "If he wants Cecelia, he can have her. Good luck to him!"

The girls never mentioned it again.

James and I didn't have much in common, and although Toi liked Caroline, they didn't become friends because Caroline always had other plans whenever Toi called her. We saw them in church every Sunday, exchanged pleasantries, and that was pretty much it.

Fast-forward a couple of months to a Sunday when James was in the pew alone.

At the end of the service, I approached him to enquire if Caroline and Luke were all right.

His eyes filled with sadness as he explained that Luke had gotten into quite a lot of trouble. He'd taken Cecelia out, and unbeknownst to him, she'd put a baggie of marijuana in his glove compartment. Later, she persuaded a waiter to serve her alcohol, and while he was driving her home, she convinced Luke to go over the speed limit, which he did to impress her. Long story short, a sheriff's deputy pulled him over for speeding, and when he went to get his registration out of the glove compartment, there was the baggie in full view of the deputy.

Luke wasn't a "bad" kid, he was just a teen who made a poor choice. He chose to pursue a friendship (of whatever sort) with a girl he didn't really know—all because she was attractive and flirtatious. He told his parents that he was just "having fun," and that is probably the truth. But choices have consequences, and Luke certainly did not like the ones he had to deal with.

Because he had no prior record, the judge was lenient: a fine and a suspended sentence with mandatory community service. Luke seemed to have learned his lesson, but the family moved soon after he fulfilled his court-mandated obligations.

This example clearly illustrates why it's important to *be selective about your friends*. But let's look at that importance from a slightly different angle.

Julie was a girl I coached in softball. I will never forget her—not because she was an outstanding athlete (she was average) but because she was an exceptional person. Truly an angel walking among us.

A week or so after tryouts, a new girl, Rilonda, joined the team. Ordinarily I didn't add members that way, but there were extenuating circumstances: Rilonda had entered the school that very week, after family services had moved her out of her abusive home. The abuse she had sustained was emotional and psychological, not physical or sexual, but the scars of that kind of abuse run deep and take a long time to heal, if ever. Rilonda's story had circulated amongst the kids, and the girls on the team didn't know quite how to interact with her.

I had spoken to the girls on the team, as had their respective teachers and the principal, but it was still awkward. Rilonda was miserable. She was also an amazingly talented athlete. I think she channeled all her anger and frustration into softball, and I felt blessed to help her in that regard.

Enter Julie, average softball player and outstanding individual.

While the other girls on the team treated Rilonda with good sportsmanship and courtesy (they knew I would tolerate nothing less), Julie reached out to her in true friendship. And she received true friendship in return. Rilonda helped Julie improve her game, and Julie restored Rilonda's faith in other humans—and in herself.

These girls were on a team I coached early on, and I stayed in touch with both of them sporadically over time. They're now in their thirties if my arithmetic is correct, and they have stayed close friends throughout all that time—through high school and college, crushes and romances, and onward into adulthood. Their friendship is still going strong. All because Julie reached out to another girl deeply in need of a friend. She saw past Rilonda's miserable façade, recognizing the hurt heart underneath. Rilonda responded to the open caring extended to her. Julie might not have known Rilonda, but she trusted her instincts and followed her heart, and that led her to make a wise choice. And that, in turn, led both girls to share a lifelong friendship— the best possible outcome of being selective about your friends.

Select How to Be Selective

There is no one way to be selective about your friends; any way that effectively works for you, and, by extension, your child(ren), is a "good" way. The trick is to make sure it truly is effective before you model it for and teach it to your kids. Everyone is different. The way we pick our friends has to work for each of us. Someone else's way might work fantastically for him or her, but be an utter disaster for you or me.

As I mentioned, we modeled being selective about choosing friends as early as we could for each of our daughters. All three girls practiced the behavior from very young ages, following their mother and me (and their older sisters; except for the eldest, of course). But Talita, Tamani, and Tylyn are individuals. We raised them with the same values and in the same household, but they are each very different people. To qualify that, I should say that they're each strong, secure, and self-assured, but each in a different way. Their personalities are not the same.

The girls were selective about their friends, but each in her own way. Talita, the eldest, chose her friends in a manner similar to the way I did (and still do). She talked to everyone, sized up each person as she considered what he or she had to say, and then she chose the ones who met her criteria for "friend": people who seemed honest, happy, and friendly—and, most important, who seemed to have integrity. (Note that I use the word *seemed*, rather than *were*, because we can only observe and attempt to discern that early in the process; many of us have been hurt and betrayed by people we knew, trusted, and loved for years.) Tamani, the middle child, chose friends in much the same way as my wife did (and still does). She met new relationships with a degree of measured skepticism, an attitude of a "prove" to me that I should allow you into my circle. For Tamani (and for Toi), this "proof" was established by the other person being direct and straightforward, displaying a certain level of seriousness that showed passion for meaningful things. Tylyn, the youngest, has always chosen friends with a combination of my penchant for friendly openness and her mom's passion for meaningful things early on in a new relationship. Toi, Tamani, and Tylyn would always say that they hated small talk. Whereas Talita and I used small talk to get to know other people, to make them feel comfortable enough to let their guard down and show us their true colors.

Again, let me reemphasize that there is no right or wrong way to do this; there is only the way that is right (or wrong) for you and your child(ren). But always remember, at the end of the day, we are the company that we keep. Remain mindful of the scripture verse opening this chapter: "He that walketh with wise [men] shall be wise: but a companion of fools shall be destroyed" (Proverb 13:20 KJV). Do not choose companions who will drag you down or keep you stuck; rather, choose people who can and will lift you up and help you grow.

Of course this should come more easily to us now as adults than it did when we were kids. We must model it for our own children so that they have positive behavior to emulate. In addition, we have to know who their friends are, how they are being raised, and how they think (or how they are taught to think). We should meet our children's friends (and their parents), engage in conversation with them, and, by all means, we should ask them questions. Don't be shy; be nosy! Make it known that you have a vested interest in getting to know them and what is happening in their lives. That vested interest is *your* child(ren). Invite your children's friends for dinner; make them feel welcome; include them in family gatherings and holiday celebrations. If the friend has a "special" title, such as boyfriend or girlfriend, explore *exactly* what that means. Terms change over time. Don't assume the meaning is the same as it was when you were that age. "Going out" doesn't necessarily mean going anywhere—at least not geographically.

Last but not least, in this the Information Age, it's easy to feel that technology has trumped us parents. I'm here to tell you that simply isn't so. No hardware, software, app, social media platform, or any instrument of technology has, can, or ever will take the place of parents. Ever. We touched on this in chapter 2, but it bears repeating. Talk to your child(ren). Spend time with your kids and their friends—at every age. Ask them questions. Listen to their answers. When they ask you questions—and they will!—give honest answers. Help them find their way by modeling the right way for them through faith-based living, through being a person of honor, integrity, and compassion. There is more to life than gadgets and the Internet. No amount of "parental controls" or "spying apps" can ever accomplish as much as caring, honesty, trust, and love can. Spying doesn't build trust or nurture love. It never has, and it never will. That said, as parents, we must serve as a sort of "firewall" for our child(ren), but we must do so by providing rock-solid reliability, trust, and love. If you raise children who feel secure, you will simultaneously raise children who find it much easier to be selective about their friends.

Now that we have seen how important it is to wisely choose our friends, let's move on to the next pages, where we will put principle number 4 into practice.

Principle #4 in Practice

Be selective about your friends.

List the people whom you consider your closest friends (if they are also members of your biological family, or if your spouse is also your best friend, indicate that next to the person's name):

_____

_____

_____

_____

Listing all the names again, describe how each person on your list contributes to your life:

_____

_____

_____

_____

Next, describe how you contribute to the life of each person on your list:

_____

_____

_____

_____

How do their contributions make you feel? How do you think your contributions make each of them feel? (If any of them have shared this with you, describe what they said):

_____

_____

_____

_____

What does principle number 4—*be selective about your friends*—mean to you?

_____

_____

_____

_____

What does the scripture verse we explored in this chapter mean to you? "He that walketh with wise [men] shall be wise: but a companion of fools shall be destroyed" (Proverb 13:20 KJV):

_____

_____

_____

Now, have your child(ren) answer the above questions in an age-appropriate manner, following the SMART system described in the introduction (and then reinforced in chapters 5 and 6), which will help make their experiences that much more meaningful.

You can use the next pages as worksheets to help you guide your child(ren) to learn and practice age-appropriate, faith-based behavior and living.

Helping Your Children Put Principle #4 in Practice
Be selective about your friends.

We've talked a lot about how important it is to choose friends carefully and wisely. Who are the people you consider your closest friends? Are any of them also your brothers, sisters, or cousins? It's okay if the answer is no! We can just talk about this, or you can write down your feelings here:

_____

_____

_____

_____

Now, let's write down all the names again, and next to each name, describe how you feel about that person. What does he or she add to your life that is really special?

_____

_____

_____

_____

Next, let's write down all the names again, but this time, describe how you think that person feels about you. What do you add to his or her life that is really special?

_____

_____

_____

_____

How do you feel about the special things that each person adds to your life? How do you think they each feel about the special things you add to their lives? If any of them have told you the answer to this, describe what they said:

_____

_____

_____

What do you think it means to *be selective about your friends*?

Let's talk about this scripture verse: "He that walketh with wise [men] shall be wise: but a companion of fools shall be destroyed" (Proverb 13:20 KJV).

What do you think that means? What do you think God wants us to do with the wisdom he gives us? We can talk about this, and you can also write down your thoughts and feelings, if you want to:

Now that we have examined why it is so important to be selective about our friends—and discussed practical ways to do so, and to teach our kids to do so as well—let's turn our attention to the next principle.

In the chapter that follows, we will explore principle number 5: *change what you need to by removing bad habits.*

Chapter 5

To put off your old self, which belongs to your former manner of life and is corrupt through deceitful desires, and to be renewed in the spirit of your minds, and to put on the new self, created after the likeness of God in true righteousness and holiness.

—Ephesians 4:22–24 ESV

Principle #5

Change what you need to by removing bad habits.

We've already acknowledged the importance of seeking truth and basing our lives on it (principle number 1), understanding who we are by knowing our family history and traditions (principle number 2), being family oriented (principle number 3), and being selective about our friends (principle number 4). Perhaps you were already aware of much of what we've discussed thus far; perhaps not. Either way, the narrative and exercises have likely caused you to think about it all more deeply, with an increased dimension, especially as it impacts your parenting and interactions with your child(ren). Certainly, that is my hope and intention.

Now it's time for me to tell you that what we've covered so far is the easy part. It's about to get harder. A lot harder. But at the end of the hard work we are embarking on, will be some of the richest rewards life has to offer: a more positive self-image, deeper and more lasting self-respect, a more effective relationship with your child(ren), and an increased and expanded sense of faith.

The first step on this harder part of the journey is understanding the concept of change, and the immediate step following that is to *change what you need to by removing bad habits*, which is the essential lesson of principle number 5.

Let's start by defining change—literally and personally—and then we can proceed to determine what we need to change (our bad habits) and how to go about doing so effectively. That is, how to accept and embrace the inevitable changes in life and also how to make positive changes that will last long-term.

What Change Is and Isn't

The *American Heritage Dictionary* defines the verb (to) *change* as "to be different," or "to cause to be different." That is the literal definition mentioned above. For each of us, *change* connotes different things; it is a word, and an action, with many nuances. It can engender a wide array of feelings, from hope and excitement, to discomfort and irritation, even anger and fear.

How many of these feelings are you experiencing right now after reading the above paragraph? Most of them? All of them? I empathize with you. Completely. I've run through the gamut of those emotions myself. Been there, done that. Whether you're laughing with me right now or squirming just thinking about the prospect of change, I have been where you are. I've felt what you're feeling. But I also bit the bullet. I did the work it took to change in the ways I needed to. I removed bad habits, and I continue to work on removing more of them. The only way to do it is to roll up your sleeves and get to work.

Before we can get to work, though, we have to know what we need to work on. To put that another way, in order to change, you have to know who you are (that means understanding principles 1 and 2). Without understanding who you are and where you come from, you can't know where you want to go, much less what you need to change! This is where the actual work takes place. This is what I call the "process." True change, lasting change, takes place during this process. The good news is, because we've already examined who we are and where we come from (in principles 1 and 2, respectively), some of the work is behind us. Now let's tackle the challenge of determining exactly what it is that we need to change.

Keep in mind that effective change will only happen—and will only last for any length of time—if it is a change that you want to have happen and are ready and willing to do the necessary work to make it happen. This might seem simple and self-evident, but it is a key point that most people miss (or ignore or overlook) during the process. Change begins, happens, and ends with you *and only you.* To a great extent, this is also true of the changes that happen because they are God's will, not ours. We cannot prevent or avoid these changes; God is always in charge, and we are just along for the ride. But it is our choice how we react to those changes. Do we accept them with grace and humility, surrendering to God's will and embracing the good he intends for us; or, conversely, do we fight those changes, with anger, bitterness, and any host of negative reactions, all of them equally impotent and purposeless?

Regardless of whether you think of it in literal terms (dictionary definition) or in terms of what it means to you personally, change is daunting. Even just *thinking* about change can be frightening. But, remember, the most important things in life will usually elicit this response; remember, too, that we all feel this way, not just you. It's hard work for each of us. It's necessary work for each of us. It's work worth doing—for each of us, and, most important of all, for our children.

The briefest explanation I can give in response to the heading of this section is that change is life; it is necessary and inevitable, and it can and does bring miracles, even when they are not evident at first. Conversely, change *isn't* avoidable, unimportant, or within our power to choose or control. Even when we recognize that we have a bad habit or self-imposed limitation that we "need to change," that isn't really our "choice" at all. It is God moving through us, saying, "The time has come. Use the intelligence and courage I gave you, and do what you need to do. Now!" Loving motivation from our Father; the same kind we give to our kids when they need it.

Before we discuss the process of change further, I'd like to share another example from my own life that illustrates the power, necessity, and inevitability of change.

The "Four Ts" of Change in My Life

When I examine my own life, I think of what I affectionately refer to as the "four Ts" of change—my wife and our three daughters. Toi, Talita, Tamani, Tylyn have completely and permanently "changed" me, each in her own way and each for the better. I wouldn't have it any other way. I am so blessed—more so than I could ever have imagined. The love I share with my wife and daughters—and now my granddaughter (hopefully the first of many grandchildren)—is at once the fulfillment of my fondest dreams and a greater blessing than any human being could create. That is the part of love that comes to us through God, whose eternal perfect love is the sum and source of all the love there is.

Throughout my life, in the course of discovering and practicing the principles in this book (1 through 7, and I go through them time and time again, just as I encourage you to do), in the course of my spiritual journey and truly getting to know my lord and savior, in the course of my personal journey of meeting and marrying my wife and raising our three daughters, I have learned, I have grown, I have loved—and, beyond all that, I have changed. Some changes I have chosen and effected; others God chose for me. Regardless, the changes were unavoidable. Even the changes I chose to make were unavoidable; I couldn't and wouldn't be the man I am today, the man I committed myself to become, if I hadn't made those changes, and, certainly, if I hadn't made the changes God decided upon.

Remember, change is inevitable. Change is life. For me, for you, for everyone.

Changing What You Need to Is Part of God's Plan for You

Consider the words of the scripture verse opening this chapter:

To put off your old self, which belongs to your former manner of life and is corrupt through deceitful desires, and to be renewed in the spirit of your minds, and to put on the new self, created after the likeness of God in true righteousness and holiness.

—Ephesians 4:22–24 ESV

When the apostle Paul put forth these words to the residents of Ephesus, especially his exhortation to the Ephesians to put off their old selves so that they could be made new, he was essentially telling them that they needed to change. In fact, he was doing so quite pointedly.

Following Paul's advice and urging, I'm suggesting the same. I believe, as I am certain he did, that God wants us to make these changes in ourselves—that is part of his loving plan for us. Because you are reading this book, I know you are leading a faith-based life. Embracing the changes God presents you with and making the changes he wants you to make are part and parcel of faith-based living, and, by extension, faith-based parenting. Similar to what we discussed above in the form of God's "pep talk" to motivate us to make the changes we need to make, and will make, through our grit and guts, and with his help, blessing, and love.

You've already read enough of this book to know that I practice what I preach. I've said more than once that I've been there myself; I empathize. I also never say "do this" without offering guidelines that will assist and support you. As with the preceding principles, I will offer some tools and tips to assist you with principle number 5—*change what you need to by removing bad habits*—but first we need to more deeply explore this challenging process.

The Process of Change: Truth, Catalysts, and Challenges

Some of us grew up in faith, and others sought and found faith as adults. Regardless of the kinds of growing-up years we had, at some point in our lives, we all received well-intentioned advice recommending that we "change for the better" and/or "get rid of bad habits." Most of us know which areas of our behavior, attitude, and/or personality could benefit from positive change. And most of us also know the bad habits we need to eliminate. In these situations, though, recognition is only the first step of a long and arduous process. It's the doing, not the knowing, that is hard. There is no way around that simple fact. Any other approach or outlook is wishful thinking, sugar-coating the hard and less-than-pleasant truth.

We already know that seeking the truth and basing your life on it is certainly essential to effective, faith-based living, but it is only the first step. In order to really live your truth, you have to know who you are, and the best way to do that is to understand where you come from. We already know that too. We've also already discovered the importance of family and choosing our friends wisely, and how both of those are also connected to faith-based living.

Have these discoveries *changed* us? Maybe yes, maybe no. That answer, if honest, is entirely individual and will vary from person to person. What is true for everyone is that life does change us, whether we recognize it or not. If you go out and do something meaningful and purposeful every day, those actions will change you. If you sit back, do nothing, and wait for meaningful and exciting things to happen to you, those actions (or inaction) will also change you. Change is inevitable. In that sense, it happens regardless of whether we want it to, regardless of whether we initiate it.

That is the kind of change that comes from God.

But what about the kind of change God want us to make? Yes, that kind of change is still part of his plan for us, but it requires us to stand up, accept the challenge, and do the work. God will fulfill the outcome, but only after we have put in the toil and sweat, the pain and tears, the commitment and energy, the love and faith.

That is the positive change we have to determine that we need to make. That is principle number 5: *change what you need to by removing bad habits.*

It is daunting, but in incremental steps, it is eminently doable. Think about the preceding chapter, where we talked about learning to be selective in choosing friends. Prior to gaining that awareness, choosing friends unwisely might have been a bad habit. So, armed with the new awareness, we can make more informed choices. Changing by removing a bad habit caused us to become wiser. The first step was awareness, the second step was determination, the third step was action, and the result was improvement.

The process is much the same with changing to remove any bad habit:

Awareness	Become aware of what you need to change.
Determination	Determine to change what you need to change.
Action	Take action on removing the bad habit you need to change.
Result	Achieve your desired improvement through your hard work, commitment, and faith—and, of course, through God's plan and love for you, which sees you successfully through all of the above!

But remember that it is a process. It takes time and effort and energy. Beyond all that, it takes faith—in yourself and in God. Remember the scripture verse opening this chapter, Paul's exhortation to the inhabitants of Ephesus:

To put off your old self, which belongs to your former manner of life and is corrupt through deceitful desires, and to be renewed in the spirit of your minds, and to put on the new self, created after the likeness of God in true righteousness and holiness.

—Ephesians 4:22–24 ESV

Can we really just "put off [our] old self"? Is it that easy? No, of course not.

Enter the catalyst. We've already discussed seeking and living our truth in previous chapters, as well as in the text above. Sometimes the changes we need to make support the truth we are already aware of; other times we need to make a change in order to embrace and practice the truth that we have suddenly discovered. Making the changes we need to make is difficult no matter what circumstances precipitate the choice to change. However, changes made in response to a truth suddenly discovered are particularly challenging. That's because this type of change is a fundamental, life-altering, 180-degree transformation. That suddenly discovered truth is what I call a "catalyst."

Catalysts take many forms. They can be some type of "religious experience," or a dramatic or tragic event, or anything that is equivalent in power to a religious awakening, a trauma, or a tragedy for any individual person. Sometimes catalysts are very instructive and helpful; other times they are extremely upsetting and painful, even terrifying. Generally, change initiated by a catalyst will force you to go outside yourself, and the only way back is to go more deeply within yourself than ever before. This outside/inside journey is the most difficult part of the process. It can be a lifelong challenge. But once that challenge is surmounted, the reward is unimaginable: you will have faced your worst demons and emerged victorious. You will be fearless. You will be free.

Before closing the narrative part of this chapter, let me clarify that my purpose in principle number 5—*change what you need to by removing bad habits*—is not to enumerate the many bad habits that plague the human race. You already know what these are, as do we all. I encourage you to use the exercises at the end of this chapter, as well as the SMART System Trackers (in this chapter and in the "Tools for Success" section in the back of this book), to help you remove the bad habits you recognize and choose to eliminate, as well as the bad habits that you need to help your child(ren) eliminate. Choosing to change by removing bad habits requires a lot of effort, as we've discussed. It requires faith, as we've also discussed. Beyond that, it requires courage. It demands guts. I know you have what it takes. God knows it too. The question is, do you know it? Do you believe it? If you don't, you should. Knowing all that it takes, you have still stepped up to the challenge. Take a moment to acknowledge yourself. Take another moment to breathe.

Take an even longer moment to pray, to ask for God's help and blessing. You are going to do this, and you are going to help your child(ren) do it too. God is with you, helping you even now; that's why you've already taken the first step by reading this far. I'm making this journey with you. Together, let's see how much further our faith can take us …

All that said, throughout this chapter we have seen how essential it is to accept and embrace God-given changes and to step up to making the changes we need to by removing bad habits, through God's will and with God's help and blessing. As stated above, now it's time to actually do the work of principle number 5: *change what you need to by removing bad habits.* That's right, the scary part, the part that makes us cringe and squirm and grumble and sweat—and sometimes even run and hide, or try to. Only now we have the tools to do it right, and that makes it less scary. So let's get to work. Let's just do it!

Principle #5 in Practice

Change what you need to by removing bad habits.

What bad habits do you need to remove? Pick at least one to work on daily. Use the SMART System Tracker at the end of this section* to log your progress:

_____

_____

_____

_____

[* There are also more SMART System Trackers in the "Tools for Success" section in the back of this book.]

Who do you talk to about your bad habit(s)? Does that person hold you accountable? If so, how? If not, who can you find who will hold you accountable?

_____

_____

_____

_____

What are some of the things that you can do to rid yourself of your bad habits?

_____

_____

_____

Commit to some action steps in order to accomplish the above:

_____

_____

_____

Add these action steps to a SMART System Tracker* but write down some thoughts about them first:

_____

_____

_____

[*You can use the one at the end of this section. There are also more SMART System Trackers in the "Tools for Success" section in the back of this book.]

What does principle number 5—*change what you need to by removing bad habits*—mean to you?

_____

_____

_____

"To put off your old self, which belongs to your former manner of life and is corrupt through deceitful desires, and to be renewed in the spirit of your minds, and to put on the new self, created after the likeness of God in true righteousness and holiness" (Ephesians 4:22–24 ESV). What does this scripture verse mean to you?

SMART[5] System Tracking
Principle #5

Change what you need to by removing bad habits.
Make All Your Changes SMART!

Specific	images, quotes, words, etc., collected for each bad habit you choose to remove
Measurable	goal set for each bad habit you choose to remove
Accountable	partner picked to help you stay committed to removing each bad habit you have determined as part of your plan to change
Realistic	each bad habit's removal is attainable, given your resources and within the time frame set by you
Time-bound	time frame established and committed to by you

Using the above system to Make All Your Changes SMART, create a SMART System Tracker that will keep you accountable for your progress as you live and practice principle number 5: *change what you need to by removing bad habits.* The SMART Tracker below will help you get started. You'll also find another SMART Tracker at the end of the next section, designed to assist you in helping your child(ren) remove bad habits. There are more of both types of trackers in the "Tools for Success" section in the back of this book.

SMART Tracker

Habit to Remove: _____

Specific	Progress	Week #	Result

Measurable	Progress	Week #	Result
Accountable	Progress	Week #	Result
Realistic	Progress	Week #	Result
Time-bound	Progress	Week #	Result

At the top of the SMART Tracker (above), write in the Habit to Remove.

Use each of the SMART boxes to ensure that you remove the bad habit according to the SMART system (Specific, Measurable, Accountable, Realistic, and Time-bound).

In the Progress boxes, mark a "+" if you were on target and a "–" if you were not on target. This will help you stay accountable, whether you are doing this on your own or with a partner.

In the Week # boxes, just indicate which week it is, to help you stay accountable.

In the Results box, indicate the outcome of having removed the bad habit.

Repeat the above steps for as long as you need to until you achieve your desired result(s). After that, move to the next habit you wish to remove and follow the same steps. Use the SMART System Trackers in the "Tools for Success" section in the back of this book.

Now, have your child(ren) answer the above questions in an age-appropriate manner, following the SMART system described in the introduction (and reinforced in this chapter and the next), which will help make their experiences that much more meaningful.

You can use the next pages as worksheets to help you guide your child(ren) to learn and practice age-appropriate, faith-based behavior and living.

Helping Your Children Put Principle #5 in Practice

Change what you need to by removing bad habits.

What is a "bad habit"? Let's talk about this, and see if you have any that you think you need to remove or work on. Pick at least one to work on daily. We'll use the SMART System Trackers at the end of this section* to log your progress, but let's write down some thoughts here to get started:

_____

_____

_____

_____

[* There are also more SMART System Trackers in the "Tools for Success" section in the back of this book.]

Who can you talk to about your bad habit(s)? You know you can always come to us, as your parents, but is there anyone else you can talk to who you think will really help you with this? If so, who, and why? How can we, your mom and dad, help?

_____

_____

_____

_____

Let's figure out some things you can start doing right now that will help you get rid of bad habits and change in ways that will help you and make you feel good:

_____

_____

_____

Now let's add these to your SMART Tracker, but we can write down some thoughts first:

_____

_____

_____

_____

What do you think it means to *change what you need to by removing bad habits?*

_____

_____

_____

Let's talk about this scripture verse: "To put off your old self, which belongs to your former manner of life and is corrupt through deceitful desires, and to be renewed in the spirit of your minds, and to put on the new self, created after the likeness of God in true righteousness and holiness" (Ephesians 4:22–24 ESV).

What do you think it means? How does God renew us in mind and spirit? We can talk about this, and you can also write down your thoughts and feelings, if you want to:

_____

_____

_____

_____

SMART[6] System Tracking
Helping Your Children with Principle #5

Change what you need to by removing bad habits.

Help Your Children Make All Changes SMART!

Specific	images, quotes, words, etc., collected for each bad habit you choose to remove
Measurable	goal set for each bad habit you choose to remove
Accountable	partner picked to help you stay committed to removing each bad habit you have determined as part of your plan to change
Realistic	each bad habit's removal is attainable, given your resources and within the time frame set by you
Time-bound	time frame established and committed to by you

Using the above system to Make All Your Changes SMART, help your child(ren) create a SMART Tracker that will keep all of you accountable for progress while living and practicing principle number 5: *change what you need to by removing bad habits.* The tracker below will help you get your child(ren) started. Follow the same system you used to complete your own tracker(s), but in an age-appropriate way for your child(ren). There are more SMART System Trackers in the "Tools for Success" section in the back of this book.

SMART Tracker

Habit to Remove: _____

Specific	Progress	Week #	Result

Measurable	Progress	Week #	Result
Accountable	Progress	Week #	Result
Realistic	Progress	Week #	Result
Time-bound	Progress	Week #	Result

[Author's Note: *The following instructions, which are the same ones that appeared with the tracker in the previous section, are designed for parents to use with their child(ren), in an age-appropriate way. They are not intended for children to use on their own.*]

At the top of the SMART Tracker (above), write in the Habit to Remove.

Use each of the SMART boxes to ensure that you remove the bad habit according to the SMART system (Specific, Measurable, Accountable, Realistic, and Time-bound).

In the Progress boxes, mark a "+" if you were on target and a "–" if you were not on target. This will help you stay accountable, whether you are doing this on your own or with a partner.

In the Week # boxes, just indicate which week it is, to help you stay

accountable.

In the Results box, indicate the outcome of having removed the bad habit.

Repeat the above steps for as long as you need to until you achieve your desired result(s). After that, move to the next habit you wish to remove and follow the same steps. Use the SMART System Trackers in the "Tools for Success" section in the back of this book.

We have gotten through the first stage of the more challenging part of the work on our journey together in faith-based parenting (and living). Now that we have examined why it is so important to change what we need to by removing bad habits—and discussed practical ways to do so, and to teach our kids to do so as well—let's turn our attention to the next principle.

In the chapter that follows, we will explore principle number 6: *do not fear failure while working toward success!*

Chapter 6

But let him ask in faith, with no doubting, for the one who doubts is like a wave of the sea that is driven and tossed by the wind. For that person must not suppose that he will receive anything from the Lord ...

—James 1:6–7 ESV

Principle #6

Do not fear failure while working toward success!

We have tackled the first phase of our more challenging work together: change and bad habits. Together, these comprise principle number 5—*change what you need to by removing bad habits.* We've seen that part of the work with change is accepting and embracing it when it is God-given and beyond our control; the other part is making the changes that we need to by removing the bad habits that don't serve us. (God intends for us to do this, but we are still the ones who have to do the work.)

Change is a never-ending process because life is always changing. It isn't the kind of thing you can do and then say, "That was hard, but at least I'm finished. I did it. I'm there." There is no *there*, not in the truest sense. And we are never really finished. But through the process of change, through doing the work, we prove to ourselves that we are strong and brave and capable, and that gives us the confidence to take on more of what we need to.

Which brings us to the next stage of the more challenging part of our journey: overcoming fear. And not just any fear, but the fear of failure. This is the lesson of principle number 6: *do not fear failure while working toward success!*

Before we begin our exploration of principle number 6, a clarification is in order. The fear discussed in this chapter is strictly the fear of failure. Fear is a huge topic—and a necessary emotion in the arsenal of human responses and reactions. We all experience what I will call "healthy fear," which alerts us to potential, and even imminent, danger. We don't want to ignore healthy fear, and we certainly don't want our children to ignore it. Children must respect healthy fear for the essential warning signal that it is. Fear of failure, on the other hand, is what I call "needless fear." Fear of failure does not help us, it hinders us. I call it "needless" because we do not need fear of failure. Fear of failure persists when we do not trust ourselves, when we lack self-confidence and self-esteem. We don't want to hold on to fear of failure, and we certainly don't want our children to hold on to it.

So now that we've clarified the difference between healthy fear and needless fear, let's keep the former for when it's needed and discard the latter because it's never needed. That's the first step toward living and practicing principle number 6: *do not fear failure while working toward success!*

Needless Fear: The Biggest Hurdle to Achieving Success

When I think about needless fear, a quote by Edmund Burke often comes to mind: "No passion so effectually robs the mind of all its powers of acting and reasoning as fear." Burke might not have qualified this statement to refer exclusively to needless fear as we've defined it, but I do. Healthy fear galvanizes us to fight and to flee; even when we are paralyzed by fear, if it is healthy, necessary fear, such paralysis can save and protect us. We stop in our tracks, and that pause can often be the difference between life and death. You get the point. It is needless fear that is destructive, eroding our peace of mind and depleting our spirits. Most important for our discussion here, this destructive aspect of needless fear is what impedes success. This is the core lesson of living and practicing principle number 6: *do not fear failure while working toward success!*

Before we can effectively examine how to avoid and/or overcome this (needless) fear of failure, we first need to discuss healthy fear a bit further. This is especially important in terms of faith-based parenting because, again, as parents, we don't ever want our children to discount or ignore healthy, necessary fear. In today's complicated world, doing so could be a recipe for disaster, tragedy, or a combination of the two.

In simplest terms, the easiest and most effective way to ensure respect for healthy, necessary fear and disregard for unhealthy, needless fear—in ourselves and our children—is to live in faith. Our awe of and trust in God is, in effect, respect for "good" fear (the healthy and necessary kind that helps to keep us safe) and renunciation of "bad" fear (the unhealthy and needless kind that impedes our success and erodes our self-esteem).

Furthermore, if we think of healthy fear as reverence for and awe toward God, we can more easily see that God intends for us to use this fear for our benefit. In other words, "healthy fear" is the awe that all the faithful possess; it is why people of faith are called "God-fearing."

Think about the scripture verse opening this chapter:

But let him ask in faith, with no doubting, for the one who doubts is like a wave of the sea that is driven and tossed by the wind. For that person must not suppose that he will receive anything from the Lord …

—James 1:6–7 ESV

This is one of many scriptural verses that illustrates the ways in which fear (that is, healthy and necessary fear) will result as a direct consequence of leaving God out of our lives, of shutting God out, of closing ourselves off to God's love and blessing. The Bible describes this innumerable times in the Old and New Testaments. In addition, the Bible offers countless instances of situations where fear results in immobilization (physical, emotional, and spiritual paralysis) that prevents and precludes calling upon God for help and accessing and utilizing divine blessing. This book is not intended to be a theological dissertation or a spiritual exegesis, but as Christians and parents desiring to model faith-based living for our children, we need to understand fear so that we can use it wisely—and teach our children to use it wisely too. For our purposes, the simple gist is this: reverence and awe (healthy, necessary fear) bring us closer to God, but immobilization and paralysis (unhealthy, needless fear) draw us farther away from God. Because God has made each and every one of us, our success and happiness and fulfillment are as important to him as they are to us—perhaps even more so. As our Father, he wants what is best for us in an even deeper and greater way than what we earthly parents want for our own children.

Examined from this perspective, we now can easily see and understand how and why needless fear prevents us from achieving the success we desire and seek: needless fear is unhealthy, and it goes against God's will and plan.

Many, many people suffer from what is often called the "fear of success." I think it is more accurate to think of this as "fear of failure," because it is too easy to shrug it off otherwise, insisting, "Fear of success? Why would I fear succeeding?"—even when that is exactly what you, and many of us, do quite frequently. Whatever phrase you prefer to apply to this pernicious affliction, we can agree that it is a needless and unhealthy fear that we must avoid and overcome by living and practicing principle number six: *do not fear failure while working toward success!*

I'd now like to share an example from my own life to illustrate the destructive potential of needless, unhealthy fear, as well as the power we can claim by overcoming that fear.

Ascending from the Middle to the Top: Achieving Success by Leaving Fear Behind

Tamani had that stereotypical "middle child syndrome." You know what I'm talking about: "*She* gets everything *her* way," was what Toi and I most often heard from Tamani during her growing-up years. It didn't matter if the *she* was her older sister (Talita) or her younger sister (Tylyn). According to Tamani, both her sisters had it easier than she did. It was always "everyone else" who picked on Tamani (and only Tamani), or said things about her that were not true, or did any number of things that caused her to feel isolated and resentful.

Psychology is not the purpose of this book, so let's set the middle child syndrome aside. Toi and I did not raise our girls to feel sorry for themselves or to cast blame. We raised them to be responsible, accountable, and caring. After I decided it was time to discover the root cause of Tamani's attitude, she did it for me.

One evening while Tamani and I were discussing her student athletic career, out came all the answers to the questions I'd been pondering.

"I hear what you're telling me, but why should I even bother? Talita will always be the track star, and Tylyn will always be the softball star. There's no place for me. I'm just noth—"

I stopped her before she could finish that last word, having none of it. "You are as good as your best shot. Same as the rest of us. If you tell me you tried your hardest and did your best, that's enough. That's everything. But to not even try because you've convinced yourself there's no point? That's not acceptable, Tamani. And it's not you."

Tamani just looked at me without saying anything. I knew it would take time to work through this issue, but I also knew I had reached her. Deep down, she knew I was right.

Even more important, I realized I had discovered the root of her problem: she was afraid to fail, so she decided the only way to avoid feeling and facing that fear was to not bother even trying to succeed!

To see the situation from Tamani's perspective, it's necessary to understand that her older sister enjoyed a very successful career as a student athlete. In fact, during her senior year in high school, Talita had many of the top colleges and universities in the country recruiting her to run track. Tylyn, a softball player, was and still is even more athletically talented than her eldest sister. (As of this writing, she is a sophomore at Stanford University, excelling in both academics and athletics.) There was Tamani, smack in the middle of her elder and younger sisters, both of whom were better athletes. To make things worse, Tamani also played softball, the sport at which her younger sister excelled.

The conversation Tamani and I had that evening proved to be quite meaningful for her. Fateful too. She could easily have just settled into the role of classic underachiever, typical middle child, working hard enough to just be good, despite her feelings of disappointment and even anger when she was not mentioned among the top athletes on her team or league. But she didn't do that. She didn't give up. She rose above the feelings that had been keeping her stuck. I helped her part of the way, talking things out with her in the ways I'd learned as a girls' softball coach. But she was the one who did the work. She found her faith—in herself, in her talent, and in recognizing exactly how much responsibility having talent entails. She matured enough to understand that God doesn't give us gifts for us to let them languish unused and unappreciated by us. Once she realized all this, she understood that fear of failure (or fear of success, if you prefer) is unhealthy and needless.

When we step up courage fills us, and then our talent flows. It just "does its thing" when we don't let needless fear get in the way. When we count on faith, we let it (and God) help us overcome the fear we don't need in the first place.

To put all this another way, the more I helped Tamani work through her issues, the more I realized the fear came in because she really wanted to be good, even great, but then she worried that would put a certain level of expectation on her. She would have to live up to that first display of greatness for the rest of her career. And if she couldn't … she simply convinced herself it would be easier to stay inside the pack than to lead the way. Blaming her sisters, or being resentful of them, was just a smokescreen. She realized that on her own, by the way.

Getting back to softball, Tamani's college career was one for the record books. She retired after a four-year career with her name penciled in the top ten in almost every offensive category. Her achievements included scoring the very first run in San Diego State's new stadium, being one of the hardest players to strike out in the country, and being called "the greatest center fielder in the history of the school" by San Diego State's play-by-play announcer.

I think it is safe to say that Tamani definitely overcame her needless fear. In fact, as soon as she stepped up and into her power, she never looked back. She went from the middle to the top, and that's where she's stayed.

As of this writing, Tamani is twenty-six years old. After completing her undergraduate work at San Diego State, she went on to get her master's degree. She is now a deputy sheriff.

As for Tamani's elder and younger sisters, Talita and Tylyn, neither one has let needless fear stand in her way. In fact, I can proudly say that all three are fearless, strong, independent women, each in her own way. Talita is now a wife and mother. For the first three years of their marriage, her husband spent at least six months of the year away from home, trying to resurrect his professional baseball career. This left Talita, a first-time mother, alone with a new baby to raise, but she did not miss a beat. She enrolled in a master of nursing program, and she's thriving as a wife, a mother, *and* a student committed to becoming a great nurse. Tylyn was probably always the most fearless of the three. When she announced that she was going to Stanford, she showed no fear whatsoever. She knew there was a lot of work to do, but she was ready, willing, and eager to do it. "Mom, Dad, it's Stanford or bust," was the way she put it. She was in third grade at the time.

So, yes, I'm proud of my daughters. They are living proof of the rewards reaped when you follow principle number 6: *do not fear failure while working toward success!*

Don't Meet Expectations, Exceed Them

Success is relevant. That might seem self-evident, but it's important to remember. Because success is relevant, don't just meet expectations—that's settling for mediocre or "just good enough"—*exceed expectations.* That is what will show *you* that you're trying your hardest, giving your all, and doing your best. For whatever that means to you. Deep down, you know. And even more important, God knows.

Society attempts to tell all of us what *success* means. It puts success in a box with many guidelines and limits, and then it tells us that if we don't reach certain steps within those guidelines, we are failures. No wonder people buy into the needless fear of failure! Worse yet, most of us in the United States are told that we can never be successful. Those who belong to any minority group receive this message from the moment they are born. So-called minority groups comprise the actual "majority" of the nation's population; nevertheless, they fall outside of societal norms. In fact, their very appearance means they will not succeed. They look "different," so how can they? Their skin color, facial features, hair color and texture, body shapes, speech patterns, dialects, accents, and beliefs all serve as reminders of this "difference," which implies an automatic inability to succeed. Those who set the "standards" have drummed this into their own heads, as well as those of the minority groups, for so long that it is pretty much considered a fact.

Well, I'm here to tell you it isn't a fact. It is a lie based on ignorance, blind hate, and needless fear. Any prejudice is always rooted in ignorance, blind hate, and needless fear. It must be overcome, and it starts with you. With each and every one of us.

The simple fact is, success has to come from within. Just as Tamani couldn't blame her own shortcomings on her sisters, neither can anyone else blame theirs on people with different skin color or different speech patterns or different beliefs. Success comes from within and from God, not from anything, or anyone, else. After all, we know that many people of all colors and creeds have attained different forms of success throughout history. Both the success that is world-renowned and the success it is personally acknowledged. In the final analysis, success is the personal declaration that your life is what you want it to be. Now that does not mean that you have all the things in life that you want, that all your worries are gone, and that you have heaven right here on earth. We all know that ain't ever gonna happen. Not in this lifetime, anyway. But those who feel successful are comfortable in their own skin; they have unshakable self-confidence and unshakable faith. They live and practice principle number 6: *do not fear failure while working toward success!*

This brings us back to the scripture verse opening this chapter:

But let him ask in faith, with no doubting, for the one who doubts is like a wave of the sea that is driven and tossed by the wind. For that person must not suppose that he will receive anything from the Lord …

—James 1:6–7 ESV

I have heard some Christians ask, "Why does bad stuff happen to me? I believe in God. I gave my life to Christ." Let me answer this as simply as I can, and remember my intention here is not to engage in theological discourse or spiritual exegesis. If you believe in God, whether you are Christian or a member of any other religion, what would God's promise to the righteous be worth if everyone were allowed to live a pain-free existence here on earth? How would God's plan to save the lost be effective if the lost could never see God at work by helping people overcome their problems? In other words, success must be measured, and, most important of all, it must be measured by a higher being. God designs our success, and then he helps us achieve it; that is why needless fear (of failure) goes against God's will and plan. No two ways about it.

To consider this in terms of someone we all recognize, let's look at the life of Earvin "Magic" Johnson. On November 7, 1991, as I was merging onto I-10 in El Monte, California, the news came on the radio that Magic was retiring because he was HIV-positive. I pulled off the interstate, stopped my car on the side of the road, and cried. I cried that warm fall morning for Magic, the Lakers, and all of mankind. There were many thoughts that raced through my head that morning, including this: "How could this happen to Magic? He is so 'successful'!"

Tragedy does not discriminate; it is the great equalizer. When I consider the Magic Johnson story now, more than twenty years later, I remember my next thought, after I stopped crying: "Man, I would not trade places with him." Supposedly, Magic had all the trappings of success. Mere weeks before that announcement, if you had asked me or anyone else to trade places with Magic Johnson, any and all of us would have jumped at the chance.

By the miracle of God's grace and medical advances, Magic Johnson is still alive more than twenty years after his initial diagnosis. Even better, he appears to be healthier than most men his age, and he is even more successful in the business world than he was in the sports world. Clearly he did not fear failure—on the court or in dealing with a life-threatening diagnosis. He stepped up, shored up his faith, and did what he had to do. I admire him tremendously. Nevertheless, when I ask myself the same question now that I asked myself then, my answer is the same: I would not trade my life and success for his. Then, I wouldn't have traded because I preferred my own ordinary existence to his tragic one, his prior success and fame notwithstanding. Now I wouldn't trade because my own ordinary existence is quite extraordinary in its own way, and because my successes, gifts, and blessings are, in a word, mine. My life is mine too. It's enough. It's everything. My sincerest wish for you is that you feel the same way about your successes, gifts, blessings, and life—for your own sake, and, even more important, for the sake of your child(ren).

In the preceding pages, we have explored the two types of fear—healthy/necessary and unhealthy/needless—and now we understand the difference between them. We live in faith, trusting and revering God, and also knowing that God alone will see us through everything, protecting us and blessing our efforts to succeed as long as we try our hardest and do our best. We also understand the relevance and blessing of success; that it is God's will and plan for us to succeed, and it is our responsibility to achieve as much success as we are able to, with his help, blessing, and love.

That said, now it's time to actually do the work of principle number 6: *do not fear failure while working toward success!*

Follow me to the next pages, where we will put principle number 6 into practice.

Principle #6 in Practice

Do not fear failure while working toward success!

How do you define *success*?

_____

_____

_____

_____

What are you doing to achieve success (as you define it)?

_____

_____

_____

_____

Do you have a timeline for achieving the success(es) you described above?

_____

_____

_____

_____

Commit to some action steps for achieving the success(es) you described above:

_____

_____

_____

_____

Add these action steps to a SMART System Tracker* but write down some thoughts about them first:

_____

_____

_____

_____

[*You can use the one at the end of this section. There are also more SMART Trackers in the "Tools for Success" section in the back of this book.]

What needless fears prevent you from achieving the success(es) you dream of?

_____

_____

_____

_____

What are you doing to overcome those needless fears?

_____

_____

_____

_____

Commit to some action steps for overcoming the needless fear(s) you described above:

_____

_____

_____

_____

Add these action steps to a SMART System Tracker* but write down some thoughts about them first:

_____

_____

_____

_____

[*You can use the one at the end of this section. There are also more SMART Trackers in the "Tools for Success" section in the back of this book.]

What does principle number 6—*do not fear failure while working toward success!*—mean to you?

_____

_____

_____

_____

What does the scripture verse we explored in this chapter mean to you? "But let him ask in faith, with no doubting, for the one who doubts is like a wave of the sea that is driven and tossed by the wind. For that person must not suppose that he will receive anything from the Lord ..." (James 1:6–7 ESV).

_____

_____

_____

_____

SMART[7] System Tracking
Principle #6

Do not fear failure while working toward success!
Make All Your Successes SMART!

Specific	images, quotes, words, etc., collected for each needless fear you choose to avoid/overcome while working toward success
Measurable	goal set for each needless fear you choose to avoid/overcome while working toward success
Accountable	partner picked to help you stay committed to avoiding/overcoming each needless fear while working toward success (determined by you as part of your plan to succeed)
Realistic	each needless fear to avoid/overcome while working toward success is attainable, given your resources and within the time frame set by you
Time-bound	time frame established and committed to by you

Using the above system to Make All Your Successes SMART, create a SMART System Tracker that will keep you accountable for progress while living and practicing principle number 6: *do not fear failure while working toward success!* The SMART Tracker below will help you get started. There are more SMART Trackers in the "Tools for Success" section in the back of this book.

SMART Tracker

Avoid/Overcome Needless Fear while Working toward Success:

Specific	Progress	Week #	Result
Measurable	Progress	Week #	Result
Accountable	Progress	Week #	Result
Realistic	Progress	Week #	Result
Time-bound	Progress	Week #	Result

At the top of the SMART Tracker (above), write in the Needless Fear to Avoid/Overcome while Working toward Success.

Use each of the SMART boxes to ensure that you avoid/overcome needless fear according to the SMART system (Specific, Measurable, Accountable, Realistic, and Time-bound).

In the Progress boxes, mark a "+" if you were on target and a "–" if you were not on target. This will help you stay accountable, whether you are doing this on your own or with a partner.

In the Week # boxes, just indicate which week it is, to help you stay

accountable.

In the Results box, indicate the outcome of having avoided/overcome fear of failure while working toward success.

Repeat the above steps for as long as you need to until you achieve your desired result(s). After that, move to the next habit you wish to remove and follow the same steps. Use the SMART System Trackers in the "Tools for Success" section in the back of this book.

Now, have your child(ren) answer the above questions in an age-appropriate manner, following the SMART system described in the introduction (and reinforced in this chapter and the previous chapter), which will help make their experiences that much more meaningful.

You can use the next pages as worksheets to help you guide your child(ren) to learn and practice age-appropriate, faith-based behavior and living.

Helping Your Children Put Principle #6 in Practice

Do not fear failure while working toward success!

Do you know what the word *success* means? Let's write down the definitions here:

_____

_____

_____

_____

What is something at which you would like to succeed?

_____

_____

_____

Why is it important to you to succeed at this?

_____

_____

_____

Let's write down some things you can do to achieve this success:

_____

_____

_____

Now let's add these to a SMART System Tracker,* but let's write down some thoughts about them first:

_____

_____

_____

_____

[*There's one at the end of this section and more in the "Tools for Success" section in the back of this book.]

Do you know what the word *failure* means? Let's write down the definitions here:

_____

_____

_____

_____

It's important to try as hard as you can to succeed, but it doesn't mean you failed if you don't succeed. Are you afraid that not succeeding will mean you failed? Why or why not?

_____

_____

_____

_____

What do you think you can do to be less afraid of failing? Can we, your mom and dad, help you? Is there another adult (teacher, pastor, coach, etc.) who can help? How?

_____

_____

_____

_____

Let's write down some things you can do to overcome the fear(s):

_____

_____

_____

Now let's add these to a SMART System Tracker,* but let's write down some thoughts about them first:

_____

_____

[*There's one at the end of this section and more in the "Tools for Success" section in the back of this book.]

Always remember that "if at first you don't succeed, try, try again!" Trying takes you at least halfway to success. As long as you know you tried your hardest and did your best, you have not failed, so *do not fear failure while working toward success!*

So now, what do you think you can do to succeed without being afraid that you might not do as well as you hope you will?

_____

_____

_____

Let's talk about this scripture verse: "But let him ask in faith, with no doubting, for the one who doubts is like a wave of the sea that is driven and tossed by the wind. For that person must not suppose that he will receive anything from the Lord ..." (James 1:6–7 ESV).

What do you think it means? How do you think God wants us to use our faith? We can talk about this, and you can also write down your thoughts and feelings, if you want to:

_____

_____

_____

SMART[8] System Tracking
Helping Your Children with Principle #6

Do not fear failure while working toward success!
Help Your Children Make All Successes SMART!

Specific	images, quotes, words, etc., collected for each needless fear you choose to avoid/overcome while working toward success
Measurable	goal set for each needless fear you choose to avoid/overcome while working toward success
Accountable	partner picked to help you stay committed to avoiding/overcoming each needless fear while working toward success (determined by you as part of your plan to succeed)
Realistic	each needless fear to avoid/overcome while working toward success is attainable, given your resources and within the time frame set by you
Time-bound	time frame established and committed to by you

Using the above system to Make All Successes SMART, help your child(ren) create a SMART System Tracker that will keep all of you accountable for progress while living and practicing principle number 6: *do not fear failure while working toward success!* The tracker below will help you get your child(ren) started. Follow the same system you used to complete your own tracker(s), but in an age-appropriate way for your child(ren). There are more SMART Trackers in the "Tools for Success" section in the back of this book.

SMART Tracker
Avoid/Overcome Needless Fear while Working toward Success:

Specific	Progress	Week #	Result
Measurable	Progress	Week #	Result
Accountable	Progress	Week #	Result
Realistic	Progress	Week #	Result
Time-bound	Progress	Week #	Result

[Author's Note: *The following instructions, which are the same ones that appeared with the tracker in the previous section, are designed for parents to use with their child(ren), in an age-appropriate way. They are not intended for children to use on their own.*]

At the top of the SMART Tracker (above), write in the Avoid/Overcome Needless Fear while Working toward Success.

Use each of the SMART boxes to ensure that you avoid/overcome needless fear according to the SMART system (Specific, Measurable,

Accountable, Realistic, and Time-bound).

In the Progress boxes, mark a "+" if you were on target and a "–" if you were not on target. This will help you stay accountable, whether you are doing this on your own or with a partner.

In the Week # boxes, just indicate which week it is, to help you stay accountable.

In the Results box, indicate the outcome of having avoided/overcome needless fear while working toward success.

Repeat the above steps for as long as you need to until you achieve your desired result(s). After that, move to the next habit you wish to remove and follow the same steps. Use the SMART System Trackers in the "Tools for Success" section in the back of this book.

We have completed the second stage of the more challenging part of the work on our journey together in faith-based parenting (and living). Now that we have examined why it is so important to not fear failure while working toward success—and discussed practical ways to do so, and to teach our kids to do so as well—let's turn our attention to the next principle.

In the chapter that follows, we will explore principle number 7: *always be yourself, but also see yourself as others see you.*

Chapter 7

And be not conformed to this world: but be ye transformed by the renewing of your mind, that ye may prove what [is] that good, and acceptable, and perfect, will of God.

—Romans 12:2 KJV

Principle #7

Always be yourself, but also see yourself as others see you.

Having now finished two of the most difficult stages of our journey—changing what we need to by removing bad habits and avoiding/overcoming needless fear while working toward success (the core lessons of principles 5 and 6, respectively)—we are ready to embark on the most challenging phase of all, the culmination of all the others preceding it. Truth to tell, we are more than ready; we are prepared by means of our discussion, exploration, and work so far.

To briefly review, we have learned how to live and practice all of the following: *seek the truth and base your life on it* (principle number 1); *know who you are by understanding your family history and traditions* (principle number 2); *be family oriented* (principle number 3); *be selective about your friends* (principle number 4); *change what you need to by removing bad habits* (principle number 5); *do not fear failure while working toward success!* (principle number 6).

Fully living and practicing these principles is an ongoing process, one we must commit to and recommit to on a daily basis. It is not the kind of thing anyone can do once and then be finished with. The principles described in this book work together synergistically; no sooner do we feel that we've "mastered" one than we find ourselves relearning another. That's just how life works. But it's also true that merely exploring principles 1 through 6 causes each of us to understand ourselves better than we ever could have before doing this work. Seeking and living our truth, understanding where we come from, eliminating our bad habits, and facing and surmounting our needless fear are not exercises for the faint of heart. We did some hard work! We were tough and brave, and we got through it. As a result, we each can say and really mean: "I know myself. I'm not perfect, but I accept who I am. I know God loves me, and I'm ready to do whatever he has planned for me. And I can handle whatever anyone else might have to say about me."

It is empowering and liberating to reach the point in life where you can say, feel, and really mean the above statement. It is an achievement for us as people and as parents. That is why we are now ready to take on what I've already described as the "hardest part": self-acceptance and self-confidence that are so unshakable they transcend and embrace the opinions of others. Really? Yes! Once we've done the work accompanying this principle, you'll see what I mean; for now, you'll just have to take my word for it.

It is now time to dive in to principle number 7: *always be yourself, but also see yourselves as others see you.*

Remember, I said "transcend and embrace the opinions of others" by means of "unshakable self-acceptance and self-confidence." That is what we must do in order to truly be ourselves—the true self sought and found and accepted and valued and loved as a result of all the discoveries made and efforts expended in the course of doing the preceding work. Let's begin our exploration of what it takes to live and practice principle number 7: *always be yourself, but also see yourselves as others see you.*

Loving the Face in the Mirror—Or, "Coming Clean"

It goes without saying that in order to really be yourself, you first have to see and accept yourself as you are. After removing bad habits (principle number 5) and facing/overcoming needless fear (principle number 6), this might sound pretty easy. It's not. It might seem easy, but it isn't. Not by a long shot. I said that I saved the hardest part for last, and I did not lie. What we are about to do is an extremely challenging exercise that I call "coming clean."

Bring a notepad and a pen or pencil into your bathroom or bedroom. Take off all of your clothes, stand in front of the mirror, and simply write down what you see. *Everything you see.* Be very specific. Write down the "good" and the "bad," the "pluses" and "minuses." You can have separate pages for "good" (pluses) and "bad" (minuses), or you can just notate your judgments next to what you write, in parentheses or in the margins. Whatever is the best and most effective way for you to do this exercise is fine.

Notice in the preceding paragraph that I used the word *judgments*. Yes, you read that correctly: this exercise is about the ways in which you judge yourself, comparing yourself to others, to your own standards for yourself and others, to the standards you have been conditioned to accept and believe, by your parents, extended family, friends, teachers, significant others, the media, and on and on. Of course this is not just about you, per se; we all live within the confines of this conditioning. We all judge ourselves, and we all judge others. That is the key to this exercise.

The trick to "coming clean" is that you will have to work hard to separate the things that you have been conditioned to believe are "good" and "bad" from your own deep-down-in-your-heart-and-soul beliefs. It's easy enough to look in the mirror and write "brown eyes." But if you have been conditioned to believe that, for example, "blue eyes are better"—or "prettier" or "nicer" or whatever descriptor comes to mind—you will naturally tag your brown eyes as "bad" or a "minus." On the other hand, if your mom and dad or an adored grandparent always complimented you on your "beautiful brown eyes," you will likely list them in your "good" section or reward them with a "plus."

I deliberately made the example simple in order to illustrate the most effective way to do this exercise. The point is, perceptions and beliefs are complicated. They are created over time, starting when we are babies and small children and lasting until we draw our last breath. Our families of origin, education system, friends, loved ones, and, of course, the media and society all contribute to our perceptions and beliefs, as well as to our opinions of ourselves.

Now you're beginning to see why I left this for last and why I said it was the hardest part! Imagine how difficult (and pointless) it would be to have done this before finding our truth, knowing where we come from, removing our bad habits, and facing and overcoming our needless fears. See? We've already done most of the legwork. So the best and most effective way to do this exercise is to draw from actual experiences with other people, and, at the same time, to be absolutely honest. To use the above example again in this context, let me ask you this: What do you think about your brown eyes? Are they "good" because you think they are "beautiful," "bright," "intelligent," etc.? Or are they "bad" because you think they are "beady," "too small," "too dark," etc.? Whatever the answer, explore how you came to that judgment. Is it something *you* really, honestly feel and believe, or are you just repeating what you have been conditioned to believe? As you answer, you'll see how much of "your" feelings and beliefs are the result of a lifetime of conditioning.

Continue "coming clean," and as you do so, delve into areas that require more emotional work than describing your eye color. Maybe you find that you have to repeat yourself because people can't hear you or find it difficult to understand you. Maybe you observe that whenever you walk into a room, everyone stops talking and turns to admire you. Or everyone else stops talking as soon as you join the conversation. Alternatively, whenever someone else tells a story, you always have a better one or have experienced a similar situation that you just have to share. Once again, you get the idea here. Describe yourself in your own words. The only thing required to do this exercise with maximum effectiveness is to be absolutely (or brutally) honest with and about yourself.

As you grow more comfortable with self-honesty, start to think in these terms when you are out in public, and make mental notes of your experience. Compare and contrast your experiences when you are with coworkers, friends, and family, and when you are with people who don't really know you. Observe what is the same (if anything) and what is different (if anything) among your interactions with different groups of people. If you travel to different cities or countries, practice this exercise in all those places. Observe and describe your experiences. It is an enlightening experience to discover a better sense of how you are viewed in the world.

This is the beginning of *seeing yourself as others see you*. But remember, it only works as the core lesson of principle number 7 if you first make and honor the commitment to *always be yourself*. Otherwise, people are not seeing the real you. Obviously, as important as this is at any age, it is most important for our children—and for us, as parents modeling effective behavior for our children, in our commitment to be faith-filled people and parents.

A final word on the "coming clean" exercise. It is only the start of living and practicing principle number 7: *always be yourself, but also see yourself as others see you*. The gathering of information that you glean through "coming clean" during your self-awareness exercises (in private) and in the mental notes you take while interacting with others (in public) is a lifelong process. The more you do it, the more you will find yourself continuously taking mental notes on how others see you. But as you do so, the judgments (about yourself and others) start to dissolve. This is where the "transcending and embracing others' opinions" takes place. Your life and your role in the world flow like water in the universe. It is truly transformational to discover this—and to live and practice it—because you will realize that this is what life is about for all humans. As living, thinking beings we are always transforming. What better behavior than that can we possibly model for our children!

To me, that is really the core message of the scripture verse opening this chapter:

And be not conformed to this world: but be ye transformed by the renewing of your mind, that ye may prove what [is] that good, and acceptable, and perfect, will of God.

—Romans 12:2 KJV

Speaking of which, here is an example of practicing principle number 7—*always be yourself, but also see yourself as others see you*—that I'd like to share from my own life.

No Room for "Crackin' and Fackin'!"—Or, Don't Conform, *Trans*form!

As I've described, Toi and Tamani are a lot alike in personality. Both are serious, direct, and no-nonsense. Most people who meet either of them for the first time have this impression: that chick does *not* mess around. As Toi likes to put it, "I am not about 'crackin' and fackin'!" In other words, she doesn't like to discuss things that are not real, as in meaningful. She doesn't enjoy sitting around making small talk or engaging in "BS"; neither does Tamani.

Now don't misunderstand me, both my wife and my middle daughter are the nicest, sweetest ladies you could ever meet, not to mention the best friends you could ever want. But a person will have to get to know them in order to discover that, and that will only happen after the protective walls come down. In terms of this principle, Toi and Tamani both have had to accept that the preceding description is most people's initial perception of them. To put this another way, they both came to see that if the majority of people they have met said things like, "I thought you were mean when I first met you," or told me things like, "man, your wife doesn't play" or "your kid is no joke," they needed to acknowledge that there was some truth in those observations and statements. Let me be clear: this did not, does not, and never will define for them who they are; nor did it, does it, or will it ever dictate who they should be. But it has, does, and will continue to help them better relate to others in the world around them, because they accept that this is who they really are and how others see them.

Having come to accept that, they had two choices: to be so affected by others' views that it resulted in the decision to change, or to acknowledge others' views without any resultant desire to change. Sometimes the former might qualify as a bad habit to remove (principle number 5), sometimes not. People often desire to change who they are in order to better fit in the world around them. As long as this does not involve denying who you are or demeaning yourself, this is fine. Many people make these kinds of changes and go on to become happy, well-adjusted people. Many make these kinds of changes, thinking that "fitting in" is the answer, only to discover that they are more miserable than they ever could have imagined. The point of principle number 7 is that the first step is to always be yourself, and the second step is to also see yourself as others see you. These steps work together to provide an honest self-image, one based on awareness and self-acceptance. And love for yourself. Based on my descriptions of Toi and Tamani throughout this book, you can pretty well guess that neither chose to just "fit in"! Instead, they have both chosen to populate their inner circles with people who "get" them, who are not intimidated by their candor and depth, who do not shrink beneath the power of their intensity.

In a way, at least where my wife is concerned, this brings me back to the question in the preface of this book: "How did you guys do it? How did you raise such faith-based, strong, amazing daughters?" Principles 1 through 7 provide the detailed answers to "how we did it." An additional answer is that Toi and I make a great team. And that relates directly to principle number 7, as outlined in the above example. I "get" Toi. I admire her serious approach to life; it is part of what I fell in love with when we first met. Pretty much as soon as I introduced myself to her, I started thinking about how much I loved the strength of this serious woman. I still feel that way.

To repeat and reemphasize the key point of this principle: seeing yourself as others see you does not mean you should change who you are for the sake of someone else, even if that someone is the person you fall in love with. Somewhere out there is the person who will "get" you, who will love you as you are and for all that you are. You must believe that for your own sake and for the sake of your child(ren), who have yet to find that person in their own lives. So live it, practice it, model it, and have faith in it. Do this every day, starting right now.

From another perspective, trying to be someone you are not is more dangerous than not understanding how you are viewed in the world. I'll use myself as an example. Knowing and understanding that, as a Black man, there will be people who will take a certain view of me simply because of the color of my skin—especially in certain parts of the world—is something I have to keep in my head at all times. Even in 2014, recognizing and remaining aware of this can literally mean the difference between life and death. I pray it will never be the center of such extreme circumstances, but it certainly does still matter in the world of business. Quite a lot, sad to say.

In my last job as a college president, I was one of only a couple of people of color on the faculty, so in meetings or at certain functions, that fact was something I could not forget, even if I'd wanted to. At one function in particular, another president of a college in our group saw me standing off to the side talking with our boss, the head of the whole group, who also happened to be Black. He walked over to us and said, "Why are you two Blacks standing over here being antisocial?" He did this even though she was his boss too, and she and I were discussing an incident that had happened at my school and that I needed her opinion on. Nevertheless, it was automatically viewed as "the two Blacks being antisocial."

Another time, when I decided to run for city council, a coworker thought it was a good thing, so she sent out an e-mail letting everyone in the company know I was volunteering to be on the city council. However, because she (without my knowledge) disseminated the information via company e-mail, our HR department required that I write an apology to the entire company. Well, of course, I took issue with this because, even if I had violated a company policy (which I hadn't, since the e-mail had not come from me), why was I being asked to write an apology? Such a requirement was not part of our progressive discipline policy. When I asked the HR representative if this was an attempt to emasculate me, the senior VP of HR retracted the request and apologized to me for his employee's having asked me to write this apology letter in the first place. And just to be clear, anyone who thinks *emasculate* is too strong a word has never experienced what it feels like to be a Black man in a white world. That is a discussion beyond the scope and intention of this book. Suffice it to say there was nothing I could do about the perceptions that cause the reaction. I am who I am, and I always will be. But that experience pointedly reminded me that no matter what position I have, I will still be Black. Period.

I accept who I am, and I also accept there will always be narrow-minded individuals. I do the best I can. So must you. So must we all. But we must never, ever allow narrow mindedness to minimize who we are and what we have to offer. We each are unique in all the universe, with something both special and specific to offer our fellow humans. That is why we're here. So find your light, and let it shine. You are here to be you. Don't be like other people just to fit in. Remember the message of principle number 7: *always be yourself, but also see yourself as others see you.* Live that, every day. Model it for your child(ren), every day. Don't conform, *trans*form! That is the way to heal the world.

All that said, we did it. We traveled through all the principles together, even the hardest one that I saved for last. We now know what it takes to be ourselves, to accept ourselves and feel confident, and yet still acknowledge the ways that others see us—for good or ill.

It's time for us to move on to the next pages, where we will put principle number 7 into practice.

Principle #7 in Practice

Always be yourself, but also see yourself as others see you.

Take a few moments to practice "coming clean." Honestly assess yourself, including your own unvarnished view and the views of others.:

_____

_____

_____

_____

Which of your own views of yourself do you feel are fair, and why? Are they positive ("good") or negative ("bad")?

_____

_____

_____

_____

Which of others' views of you do you feel are fair, and why? Are they positive ("good") or negative ("bad")?

_____

_____

_____

_____

Are any of these fair and honest views things that you choose to change? Why or why not?

_____

_____

_____

_____

[Author's Note: *If you choose to make changes, follow the steps in chapter 5. If you choose not to, be sure that it is because you accept yourself as you are and don't feel that you need to change. Sometimes fear of change is like fear of success—don't fall into the trap of needless fear, which you must always avoid and/or overcome. If you aren't sure, review chapter 6. You can always work through either or both experiences on a SMART Tracker (see the "Tools for Success" section in the back of this book).]*

What does principle number 7—*always be yourself, but also see yourself as others see you*—mean to you?

_____

_____

_____

_____

What does the scripture verse we explored in this chapter mean to you? "And be not conformed to this world: but be ye transformed by the renewing of your mind, that ye may prove what [is] that good, and acceptable, and perfect, will of God" (Romans 12:2 KJV).

_____

_____

_____

_____

Now have your child(ren) answer the above questions in an age-appropriate manner, following the SMART system described in the introduction (and reinforced in the previous two chapters), which will help make their experiences that much more meaningful.

You can use the next pages as worksheets to help you guide your child(ren) to learn and practice age-appropriate, faith-based behavior and living.

Helping Your Children Put Principle #7 in Practice

Always be yourself, but also see yourself as others see you.

Let's talk about what you think is special about you, how you think about yourself, and how others see you too. We can just talk about this, and you can also write down your feelings here:

Which of your own views of you do you feel are fair, and why? Are they positive ("good") or negative ("bad")?

Which of others' views of you do you feel are fair, and why? Are they positive ("good") or negative ("bad")?

Are any of these fair and honest views things that you choose to change? Why or why not?

[Author's Note: *If you choose to encourage your child(ren) to make changes, follow the steps in chapter 5. If you choose not to, be sure that it is because your child(ren) are truly self-accepting and don't feel the need to change—and that you do not feel there is a need for positive change in this area, especially if it relates to safety and/or well-being. Sometimes fear of change is like fear of success. Don't let your child(ren) fall into the trap of needless fear, which you must guide them to always avoid and/or overcome. If you aren't sure, review chapter 6. You can always work together through either or both experiences on a SMART Tracker (see the "Tools for Success" section in the back of this book).]*

What do you think this means to *always be yourself, but also see yourself as others see you?*

Let's talk about this scripture verse: "And be not conformed to this world: but be ye transformed by the renewing of your mind, that ye may prove what [is] that good, and acceptable, and perfect, will of God" (Romans 12:2 KJV).

What do you think it means? How do you think God wants us to transform so that we can do his will? We can talk about this, and you can also write down your thoughts and feelings, if you want to:

We have finished the third and final stage of the more challenging part of the work on our journey together in faith-based parenting (and living). Now that we have examined why it is so important to always be yourself, but also to see yourself as others see you—and discussed practical ways to do so, and to teach our kids to do so as well—it's time for us to review what we've learned together.

Having explored all the principles, 1 through 7, in great detail, let's move on to the conclusion and "Tools for Success" sections, where we will summarize our discussion, and where you will have the opportunity to use and further explore even more ways to model faith-based behavior and practice faith-based parenting.

Conclusion

I can do all things through him who strengthens me.

—Philippians 4:13 ESV

As discussed throughout this book, parenting based on Christian values is the key to raising happy and successful children. The 7 principles I have developed and shared with you will help you achieve that. However, remember that I didn't invent those principles, God did. I simply found an effective way to use the principles in daily life and to teach my three daughters to do the same.

As stated in the introduction, the secret is that it isn't a secret at all. It is unshakable faith in our God. Toi and I communicated that faith to our daughters, and they succeeded because of it. We raised our three daughters to love God, to love themselves, and to love other people. Over time, we felt the results of our parenting were very successful, leading people to ask us, "How did you guys do it?"

I hope this book has provided sufficient answers to that question; I certainly intended for it to do so. Beyond that, my goal was to create a perennial one-stop reference for Christian parents to use again and again, and I hope you will feel that I have succeeded.

Remember that I promised this book would offer tools and tips to help make faith work for you, and to provide you with the tools necessary to create a practical application of spiritual belief.

To keep them fresh in our minds, here are the 7 principles we've thoroughly explored throughout the chapters of this book:

The 7 Principles of Faith-Based Parenting

1. Seek the truth, and base your life on it.

2. Understand who you are by knowing your family history and traditions.

3. Be family oriented.

4. Be selective about your friends.

5. Change what you need to by removing bad habits.

6. Do not fear failure while working toward success.

7.   Always be yourself, but also see yourself as others see you.

As I've said before, what we get out of the principles' lessons depends on our individual points in life's journey, our own relationship with God, and our faith. But remember, this is a book you can reread as many times as needed, and I hope you will do exactly that. Most of all, I hope this book will enhance your experience of living—and parenting—in faith and with God's help, blessing, and eternal love.

And now, as I did in the preface, I'd like to share some more of my three daughters' insights.

In My Daughters' Own Words

I asked each of my daughters two questions as I came to the end of the process of writing this book:

1.   Why are you focused the way you are?

2.   Where did this focus come from that makes you different from other family members?

Following are the answers to the above two questions, in each of my three daughters' own words.

Talita

Dad, I love you and thank you! My answers to the questions you asked are kind of blended together, but here they are:

To start, there is a quote from Marianne Williamson's *A Return to Love* that I like to remind myself of often:

Our deepest fear is not that we are inadequate. Our deepest fear is that we are powerful beyond measure. It is our light, not our darkness that most frightens us. We ask ourselves, 'Who am I to be brilliant, gorgeous, talented, fabulous? Actually, who are you not to be? You are a child of God. You're playing small does not serve the world. There is nothing enlightened about shrinking so that other people won't feel insecure around you. We are all meant to shine, as children do. We were born to make manifest the glory of God that is within us. It's not just in some of us; it's in everyone. And as we let our own light shine, we unconsciously give other people permission to do the same. As we are liberated from our own fear, our presence automatically liberates others.

I wholly know God sees us not for who we are at this moment but for our potential and for all that we can be and do. He has plans for our future, as the Bible tells us: "For I know the plans I have for you, declares the LORD, plans for welfare [peace] and not for evil, to give you a future and a hope" (Jeremiah 29:11 ESV).

I want to see myself as God sees me. And I need to honor him for the talents and gifts he has given me. Who am I not to be successful? I am a child of God, and I am powerful beyond measure.

Admittedly, though, it is hard work, and I am not always super encouraged. Sometimes I get sidetracked, distracted, disappointed, and struck down by the details of the circumstances. But then I remember God won't take me anywhere he is not waiting for me already. This does not mean everything will be a walk in the park. Actually, I think it means it definitely *won't* be a walk in the park; it means I can't do anything in my own strength alone. No one can. God works through people, and he has set up people and relationships to support each one of us. And I, like everyone else, have to have faith.

I used to think that "it" was about having a lot of faith versus no faith. I now realize that everyone has faith. What we each place our faith *in* is the question, along with the duration of that faith. Faith in anything other than God and his gifts and blessings will never last or be completely reliable. Also, it's not enough to have tremendous faith for just five seconds, even if that faith is in God. What we each need is a little faith in God that we nurture every day so it will last forever!

A big part of my focus is that I want to make a difference. A freaking huge, amazing, big difference. The way I envision myself doing this is by serving people in the health-care field. This is what I am passionate about doing. I have been on the administrative side for years, but I want to *directly* make a difference, with my hands and my spirit! As I pursue my nursing degree and licensure, I am determined to be successful in school and otherwise, simply because I care and have empathy. I work hard because if I were in my helper's shoes, I would want the person helping me to be wholly committed to his or her work, role, and responsibility. I would want to know that he or she prepared for this moment the best way possible and is the most appropriate person for this. Would I want a mediocre person helping me, someone who wasn't fully committed? Absolutely not!

I also work hard and want to be successful because I have an obligation to be the best I can for my husband and our daughter, who is now three years old. You and Mom were that for me, and I am forever indebted to both of you for that. I cannot say I fully even know all of the sacrifices you made for me and my sisters, but I can tell you none of us three girls would be who we are today without *both* of you! We are so utterly blessed! And you know what? You and Mom continue to inspire me. You work tirelessly, believe in yourselves and each other, pursue God with fervor, laugh a lot, and have a healthy marriage. I want all that for my daughter and any future children my husband and I have.

Tamani

Thanks for asking me, Dad. I am focused on being successful because reaching my goals and being productive is what gives me a good feeling. You and Mom loved me and were good role models for me throughout my life. Even more important, you taught me how to keep good, positive people around me, to help and encourage me to be successful.

You raised my sisters and me to believe in God and to believe we were special. We believe God has given us our talents or gifts. Quitting or giving up on our gifts was not okay. It's still not okay.

The main difference between us and other family members is probably how we were raised and what stimulates us. We were raised to always do positive things and to know the difference between right and wrong, black and white. Some people were taught to look out for number 1 no matter what—by cheating, lying, stealing, and whatever other means. They always put themselves first and never think about other people. They will ask others to give their last dollar, but they wouldn't ever do a thing to help another person or to give away what they think they, and only they, deserve and are entitled to. Then again, maybe they really don't think they deserve better, so they limit themselves in order to not feel worse about themselves. Kind of like, if you don't dream big, you won't fail big. Maybe they weren't taught to dream at all.

You and Mom taught us to dream, to help others, and to have faith in God. I still do all that to this very day. It makes me a good at my job in law enforcement, and it makes me feel good about who I am too.

Tylyn

Hi, Dad. I am so focused on school and being successful because I understand I have the ability to do well and to succeed. I know I am intelligent. I know I can be creative. I know I can accomplish so much.

You and Mom are the reason why I feel this way. You made it very clear to my sisters and me that we were capable, and you expected us to show our capability. You always want the best for us, so naturally I want the best for myself.

Remember when I set my sights on Stanford? I think I was about eight years old, but I remember how good I felt about it. How clear and focused. I knew I could and would do it, and I have! And I know I can and will do even more.

*

Talita, Tamani, and Tylyn did not specifically mention the 7 principles in any of their responses to my questions, but they lived and practiced them every day growing up—Toi and I saw to that. They still live and practice them every day; the principles are second nature to them now, just as they are to Toi and me, and just as they will be to you and your child(ren).

That said, let's move on to the "Tools for Success" section, where you can put the practical application of the 7 principles to work!

[Author's Note: *The "Tools for Success" section contains additional exercises and resources. You can utilize these as many times as you wish in the future. As stated throughout this book, my ultimate goal is for this book to become a perennial resource for you as a parent, all throughout the growing-up years of your child(ren).*]

Tools for Success

We've talked about the "Tools for Success" section throughout this book. As promised, this section provides various types of exercises for you and your child(ren) to use in order to integrate each of the 7 principles into your daily lives—and to live in faith and be as happy and successful as God intends.

There are pages that revisit the "Principles in Practice" sections from each chapter (both parents' and children's versions). These will enhance and reinforce what we have already explored in the chapters, helping you derive even more meaning and purpose from using the 7 principles. Follow the same process with these as you did in the chapters.

There are also pages that revisit the SMART System, including more SMART System Trackers (both parents' and children's versions). You can use these to create positive change(s), achieve success(es), and learn, grow, and heal in whatever other area(s) you deem appropriate. There are also SMART System Trackers designed specifically for use with dreams and goals (as described in the introduction). Follow the same process with these as you did in the chapters.

Finally, there are Guided Journaling pages (both parents' and children's versions) centered on each of the 7 principles and each of the scripture verses opening the chapters and the conclusion.

Let me reemphasize that I recommend you use the "Tools for Success" exercises and resources over and over, throughout the growing-up years of your child(ren). Help them use the tools in age-appropriate ways, with your guidance and following the faith-based living you model for them using the 7 principles discussed throughout this book.

And now let's proceed to using those tools!

Principles in Practice: "Use Them or Lose Them!"

This section provides additional pages for you to use to put the 7 principles in practice on a daily basis—and to guide your child(ren) to do so as well, in age-appropriate ways. Now that we have discussed all 7 principles, the answers to these exercises might change when you do them again. The same might be true for your child(ren).

Over time and after using the principles ongoing, it is always effective to do the exercises again. Please return here as often as needed and desired, and recommit to putting all 7 principles into practice throughout your life and the growing-up years of your child(ren). Remember, follow the same process with these as you did in the chapters.

What's true in so many other contexts is equally true of the 7 principles: use them or lose them!

[Author's Note: *The Guided Journaling pages offer space for you to more deeply explore your thoughts and feelings related to each of the 7 principles and the scripture verse opening each chapter and the conclusion. There are also Guided Journaling pages for you to use with your child(ren) to more deeply explore each of the 7 principles and scripture verses, in age-appropriate ways.*]

Revisiting Principle #1 in Practice

Seek the truth, and base your life on it.

Now that we have gone through all 7 principles, once again think about the situations in your life that have challenged a foundation of truth you were taught.

Write down what they were:

_____

_____

_____

_____

Given what you've learned in this book, do you feel differently about how these situations affected you? Why or why not?

_____

_____

_____

_____

After reading this book, have you made any additional changes in your life? Why or why not?

_____

_____

_____

_____

If so, how have these changed or affected you?

_____

_____

_____

_____

Revisiting Helping Your Children Put Principle #1 in Practice

Seek the truth, and base your life on it.

Let's talk some more about how to seek the truth and then live our lives based on it. We've done this before, and it's a pretty big job. Let's do it again, though, because it's important. We can start by talking about things that have happened that have made you wonder about what was and wasn't true.

We can just talk about them, or you can write them down here:

_____

_____

_____

_____

How did you feel about this? Did it make you feel scared, mad, ashamed, or any other feeling?

_____

_____

_____

What things should we change because of this? Can we change them? Why or why not?

_____

_____

_____

_____

What has happened because of these changes, or because of no changes?

_____

_____

_____

_____

Revisiting Principle #2 in Practice

Understand who you are by knowing your family history and traditions.

You can fill out this additional family tree if you wish:

Family Tree

_____ & _____   _____ & _____

_____ & _____   _____ & _____

_____ & _____

_____   _____   _____

_____

Now that we've gone through all 7 principles, think about your place in your family. (You can fill out another family tree if you wish.) Write down how you feel about your place in the family. How did being the eldest/youngest/middle/etc., affect you? Have your answers changed since last time? Why or why not?

_____

_____

_____

_____

List the people from your family of origin (and/or from your extended family) who touched your life. Have your answers changed since last time? Why or why not?

Find a way to personally thank each of them. (Remember, those who have passed on you can still thank through prayer.) You can do this as many times throughout your life as feels meaningful to you.

_____

_____

_____

_____

After reading this book, create a tradition for you and your immediate family, and then share it with your existing community. You can do this again and again.

_____

_____

_____

_____

Revisiting Helping Your Children Put Principle #2 in Practice

Understand who you are by knowing your family history and traditions.

<u>Family Tree</u>

_____ & _____   _____ & _____

_____ & _____   _____ & _____

_____ & _____

_____   _____   _____

_____

Remember the family tree we did? We can do another one, or we can just talk about it. How do you feel about being the oldest/middle/youngest/etc.? You can write down your feelings here if you want to:

_____

_____

_____

Since we last talked about this, who in our family has really made a big difference in your life? Remember, it's okay—you don't have to say Mom or Dad!

_____

_____

_____

Let's think of some more special ways to thank _____ (fill in the name[s] of those listed above):

_____

_____

_____

_____

Since we last talked about it, what traditions do we have as a family that you like or don't like?

_____

_____

_____

_____

Let's make some more new traditions! We can even share them with our friends and people we know in the community:

_____

_____

_____

_____

Revisiting Principle #3 in Practice

Be family oriented.

You can fill out this additional family tree if you wish:

Family Tree

_____ & _____   _____ & _____

_____ & _____   _____ & _____

_____ & _____

_____   _____   _____

_____

Based on reading this book, once again think about the biological family relationships that you have. Are they the way you would like them to be? Why or why not? How have your answers changed since last time?

_____

_____

_____

After reading this book, describe some more ways in which you can make these relationships better, or at least more in line with the way you would like them to be:

_____

_____

_____

Commit to some new action steps to make the changes described above:

_____

_____

_____

_____

Has your social family changed since you read this book? Why or why not?

_____

_____

_____

Have your community (social family) responsibilities changed since you read this book? Why or why not? If you still don't have any community responsibilities, how can you find a way to reach out to your community?

_____

_____

_____

Commit to some new action steps to make the changes described above:

_____

_____

_____

Describe some of the ways in which you can improve or enhance your existing social relationships, based on what you have learned in this book:

_____

_____

_____

Commit to some action steps to make the changes described above:

_____

_____

_____

Revisiting Helping Your Children Put Principle #3 in Practice

Be family oriented.

Remember the family tree we did? Let's do another one!

<u>Family Tree</u>

_____ & _____   _____ & _____

_____ , & _____   _____ & _____

_____ & _____

_____   _____   _____

_____

Think about our family once again. Is everything the way you would like it to be? Why or why not? We can talk about this, or you can write down your feelings here:

_____

_____

_____

How have things changed since last time? Can we make any of these things better, or at least more like you wish they could be?

_____

_____

_____

Let's do these new things, and see if we can make the changes happen:

_____

_____

_____

Do you have any friends at school or on teams or in church who feel like family to you? Have your answers changed since last time? Why or why not?

_____

_____

_____

What jobs do you have at home or at school or on your team or in church? If you don't have any, would you like some? Why or why not? How have your feelings about this changed since the last time we talked about it?

_____

_____

_____

Let's figure out how you can take on some jobs or add some new ones:

_____

_____

_____

Do you think you can be a better friend or teammate? Why or why not? How have your answers changed since last time?

_____

_____

_____

If you still want to be a better friend or teammate, let's figure out how you can do it:

_____

_____

Revisiting Principle #4 in Practice

Be selective about your friends.

After reading this book, list the people whom you consider to be your closest friends (if they are also members of your biological family, or if your spouse is also your best friend, indicate that next to the person's name). How have your answers changed since last time?

_____

_____

_____

_____

Listing all the names again, describe how each person on your list contributes to your life. How have your answers changed since last time?

_____

_____

_____

_____

Next, describe how you contribute to the life of each person on your list. How have your answers changed since last time?

_____

_____

_____

_____

How do their contributions make you feel? How do you think your contributions make each of them feel? (If any of them have shared this with you, describe what they said.) How have your answers changed since last time?

_____

_____

_____

_____

Revisiting Helping Your Children Put Principle #4 in Practice

Be selective about your friends.

We've talked a lot about how important it is to choose friends carefully and wisely. Let's talk about some more, though, because it's important.

Who are the people you consider to be your closest friends? Are any of them also your brothers, sisters, or cousins? It's okay if the answer is no! How have your answers changed since last time?

We can just talk about this, or you can write down your feelings here:

_____

_____

_____

_____

Now, let's write down all the names again, and next to each name, describe how you feel about that person. What does he or she add to your life that is really special? How have your answers changed since last time?

_____

_____

_____

_____

Next, let's write down all the names again, but this time, describe how you think that person feels about you. What do you add to his or her life that is really special? How have your answers changed since last time?

_____

_____

_____

_____

How do you feel about the special things that each person adds to your life? How do you think they each feel about the special things you add to their lives? If any of them have told you the answer to this, describe what they said. How have your answers changed since last time?

Revisiting Principle #5 in Practice

Change what you need to by removing bad habits.

What bad habits do you need to remove? Pick at least one to work on daily. How have your answers changed since last time? Use the SMART System Tracker in "The SMART System, Revisited" to log your progress:

_____

_____

_____

_____

Now that we've gone through all 7 principles, who do you talk to about your bad habit(s)? Does that person hold you accountable? If so, how? If not, who can you find who will hold you accountable? How have your answers changed since last time?

_____

_____

_____

_____

Having studied all 7 principles, what are some of the things that you can do to rid yourself of your bad habits? How have your answers changed since last time?

_____

_____

_____

_____

Commit to some new action steps in order to accomplish the above:

_____

_____

_____

_____

Add these new action steps to a SMART System Tracker* but write down some thoughts about them first:

_____

_____

_____

_____

[*You'll find more trackers in "The SMART System, Revisited."]

Revisiting Helping Your Children Put Principle #5 in Practice

Change what you need to by removing bad habits.

We've talked about "bad habits." Since we last talked, do you think you need to remove or work on any new ones? Pick at least one to work on daily. We'll use SMART System Trackers* to log your progress, but we can talk about or write down some thoughts now if you want to:

_____

_____

_____

[*There are more trackers in "The SMART System, Revisited."]

Who can you talk to about your bad habit(s)? You know you can always come to us, as your parents, but is there anyone else you can talk to who you think will really help you with this? If so, who, and why? How can we, your mom and dad, help? How have your answers changed since last time?

_____

_____

_____

Let's figure out some more things you can start doing right now that will help you get rid of bad habits and change in ways that will help you and make you feel good:

_____

_____

_____

Now let's add these to your SMART Tracker, but let's write down some thoughts about them first:

_____

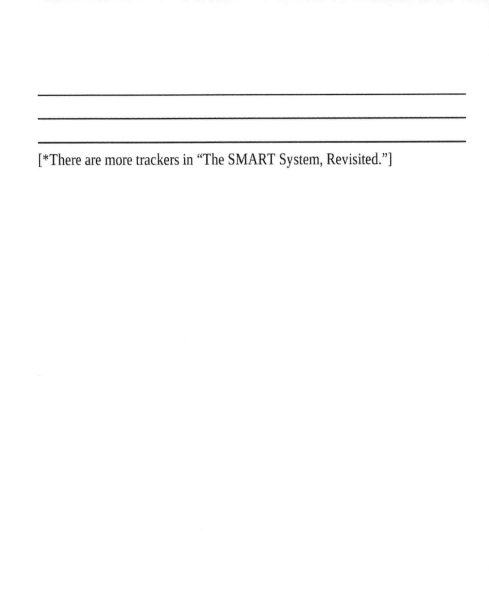

[*There are more trackers in "The SMART System, Revisited."]

Revisiting Principle #6 in Practice

Do not fear failure while working toward success!

Now that you've read this book, how do you define *success*? Has your definition changed since last time? Why or why not?

_____

_____

_____

_____

What are you doing to achieve success (as you define it)? How have your answers changed since last time?

_____

_____

_____

_____

Do you have a timeline for achieving the success(es) you described above? How have your answers changed since last time?

_____

_____

_____

_____

Commit to some new action steps for achieving the success(es) you described above:

_____

_____

_____

_____

Add these action steps to a SMART System Tracker,* but write down some thoughts about them first:

_____

_____

[*You'll find more trackers in "The SMART System, Revisited."]

Since reading this book, what needless fears prevent you from achieving the success(es) you dream of? How have your answers changed since last time?

What are you now doing to overcome those needless fears? How have your answers changed since last time?

Commit to some new action steps for overcoming the needless fear(s) you described above:

Add these action steps to a SMART System Tracker,* but write down some thoughts about them first:

[*You'll find more trackers in "The SMART System, Revisited."]

Revisiting Helping Your Children Put Principle #6 in Practice

Do not fear failure while working toward success!

We've talked about what the word *success* means. Let's write down some definitions. How have these changed since we last talked about this?

_____

_____

_____

_____

Since we last talked about this, what is something you would like to succeed at?

_____

_____

_____

_____

Why is it important to you to succeed at this?

_____

_____

_____

_____

Let's write down some things you can do to achieve this new success:

_____

_____

_____

_____

Now let's add these to a SMART System Tracker,* but let's write down some thoughts about them first:

_____

_____

_____

_____

[*There are more trackers in "The SMART System, Revisited."]

We've talked about what the word *failure* means. Let's write down the definitions here. How have these changed since we last talked about this?

_____

_____

_____

Remember, it's important to try as hard as you can to succeed, but it doesn't mean that you failed if you don't succeed. Are you still afraid that not succeeding will mean that you failed? Why or why not? How have your answers changed since last time?

_____

_____

_____

Now that we've talked about it more, what do you think you can do to be less afraid of failing? Can we, your mom and dad, help you? Is there another adult (teacher, pastor, coach, etc.) who can help? How? Have your answers changed since last time? Why or why not?

_____

_____

_____

Let's write down some new things you can do to overcome the fear(s):

_____

_____

_____

Now let's add these to a SMART System Tracker,* but let's write down some thoughts about them first:

_____

_____

_____

_____

[*There are more trackers in "The SMART System, Revisited."]

Revisiting Principle #7 in Practice

Always be yourself, but also see yourself as others see you.

Once again, take a few moments to practice "coming clean." Honestly assess yourself, including your own unvarnished view and the views of others. Have your answers changed since last time? Why or why not?

_____

_____

_____

_____

After further reading, which of your own views of yourself do you feel are fair, and why? Are they positive ("good") or negative ("bad")? Have your answers changed since last time? Why or why not?

_____

_____

_____

_____

After reading, which of others' views of you do you feel are fair, and why? Are they positive ("good") or negative ("bad")? Have your answers changed since last time? Why or why not?

_____

_____

_____

_____

After reading, are any of these fair and honest views things that you choose to change? Why or why not? How have your answers changed since last time?

_____

_____

_____

_____

[Author's Note: *As discussed in chapter 7, if you choose to make changes, follow the steps in chapter 5. If you choose not to, be sure that it is because you accept yourself as you are and don't feel that you need to change. Sometimes fear of change is like fear of success—don't fall into the trap of needless fear, which you must always avoid and/or overcome. If you aren't sure, review chapter 6. You can always work through either or both experiences on a SMART Tracker. There are additional SMART Trackers in the "SMART System, Revisited."*]

Revisiting Helping Your Children Put Principle #7 in Practice

Always be yourself, but also see yourself as others see you.

Let's talk some more about what you think is special about you, how you think about yourself, and how others see you too. We can just talk about this, and you can also write down your feelings here. How have your answers changed since last time?

_____

_____

_____

_____

Which of your own views of you do you feel are fair, and why? Are they positive ("good") or negative ("bad")? How have your answers changed since last time?

_____

_____

_____

_____

Which of others' views of you do you feel are fair, and why? Are they positive ("good") or negative ("bad")? How have your answers changed since last time?

_____

_____

_____

_____

Are any of these fair and honest views things that you choose to change? Why or why not? How have your answers changed since last time?

_____

_____

[Author's Note: *As discussed in chapter 7, if you choose to encourage your child(ren) to make changes, follow the steps in chapter 5. If you choose not to, be sure that it is because your child(ren) are truly self-accepting and don't feel the need to change—and that you do not feel there is a need for positive change in this area, especially if it relates to safety and/or well-being. Sometimes fear of change is like fear of success. Don't let your child(ren) fall into the trap of needless fear, which you must guide them to always avoid and/or overcome. If you aren't sure, review chapter 6. You can always work together through either or both experiences on a SMART Tracker. There are additional SMART Trackers in the "SMART System, Revisited."*]

The SMART[9] System, Revisited

As mentioned in a footnote in the introduction, the first usage of SMART was in the early 1980s, and it was based on Peter Drucker's management concepts. Throughout the thirty-plus years since then, SMART has been used in many situations and across a wide array of industries and disciplines, both within and outside the business world—all with the intent of helping people create a goal system that would enable them to become the most effective people they could be.

Throughout this book, we've discussed the SMART system, as well as the SMART Trackers I recommend you use to implement the 7 principles in your daily life. The pages that follow revisit the SMART System, including more SMART System Trackers (both parents' and children's versions). You can use these to create positive change(s) (e.g., principle number 5: *change what you need to by removing bad habits*), achieve success(es) (e.g., principle number 6: *do not fear failure while working toward success!*), and learn, grow, and heal in whatever other area(s) you deem appropriate. There are also SMART System Trackers designed specifically for use with dreams and goals (as described in the introduction).

Let's begin by revisiting the SMART System Trackers (both parents' and children's versions) for creating positive change(s) and achieving successes. We will then move to the SMART Trackers for goals/dreams, and after that, there will be SMART Trackers for you to use as desired. Again, follow the same process with these as you did in the chapters.

Revisiting the SMART[10] System Tracker for Positive Changes

Principle #5: Change what you need to by removing bad habits

Make All Your Changes SMART!

Specific	images, quotes, words, etc., collected for each bad habit you choose to remove
Measurable	goal set for each bad habit you choose to remove
Accountable	partner picked to help you stay committed to removing each bad habit you have determined as part of your plan to change
Realistic	each bad habit's removal is attainable, given your resources and within the time frame set by you
Time-bound	time frame established and committed to by you

As discussed in chapter 5, using the above system to Make All Your Changes SMART, create a SMART System Tracker that will keep you accountable for your progress as you live and practice principle number 5: *change what you need to by removing bad habits.* The SMART Tracker below will help you get started. You'll also find another SMART Tracker after this one, designed to assist you in helping your child(ren) remove bad habits.

SMART Tracker

Habit to Remove: _____

Specific	Progress	Week #	Result

Measurable	Progress	Week #	Result
Accountable	Progress	Week #	Result
Realistic	Progress	Week #	Result
Time-bound	Progress	Week #	Result

As explained in chapter 5, at the top of the SMART Tracker (above), write in the Habit to Remove.

Use each of the SMART boxes to ensure that you remove the bad habit according to the SMART system (Specific, Measurable, Accountable, Realistic, and Time-bound).

In the Progress boxes, mark a "+" if you were on target and a "–" if you were not on target. This will help you stay accountable, whether you are doing this on your own or with a partner.

In the Week # boxes, just indicate which week it is, to help you stay accountable.

In the Results box, indicate the outcome of having removed the bad habit.

Repeat the above steps for as long as you need to until you achieve your desired result(s). After that, move to the next habit you wish to remove and follow the same steps. Make your own SMART System Trackers to use on as many bad habits as you need to remove.

Revisiting Helping Your Children with the SMART[11] System Tracker for Positive Changes

Principle #5: Change what you need to by removing bad habits

Help Your Children Make All Changes SMART!

Specific	images, quotes, words, etc., collected for each bad habit you choose to remove
Measurable	goal set for each bad habit you choose to remove
Accountable	partner picked to help you stay committed to removing each bad habit you have determined as part of your plan to change
Realistic	each bad habit's removal is attainable, given your resources and within the time frame set by you
Time-bound	time frame established and committed to by you

As discussed in chapter 5, using the above system to Make All Changes SMART, help your child(ren) create a SMART Tracker that will keep all of you accountable for progress while living and practicing principle number 5: *change what you need to by removing bad habits.* The tracker below will help you get your child(ren) started. Follow the same system you used to complete your own tracker(s), but in an age-appropriate way for your child(ren).

SMART Tracker

Habit to Remove: _____

Specific	Progress	Week #	Result

Measurable	Progress	Week #	Result
Accountable	Progress	Week #	Result
Realistic	Progress	Week #	Result
Time-bound	Progress	Week #	Result

[Author's Note: *The following instructions, which are the same ones that appeared with the tracker in the previous section, are designed for parents to use with their child(ren), in an age-appropriate way. They are not intended for children to use on their own.*]

As discussed in chapter 5, at the top of the SMART Tracker (above), write in the Habit to Remove.

Use each of the SMART boxes to ensure that you remove the bad habit according to the SMART system (Specific, Measurable, Accountable, Realistic, and Time-bound).

In the Progress boxes, mark a "+" if you were on target and a "–" if you were not on target. This will help you stay accountable, whether you are doing this on your own or with a partner.

In the Week # boxes, just indicate which week it is, to help you stay

accountable.

In the Results box, indicate the outcome of having removed the bad habit.

Repeat the above steps for as long as you need to until you achieve your desired result(s). After that, move to the next habit you wish to remove and follow the same steps. Make your own SMART System Trackers to use on as many bad habits as you need to help your child(ren) remove.

Revisiting the SMART[12] System Tracker for Success

Principle #6: Do not fear failure while working toward success!

Make All Your Successes SMART!

Specific	images, quotes, words, etc., collected for each needless fear you choose to avoid/overcome while working toward success
Measurable '	goal set for each needless fear you choose to avoid/overcome while working toward success
Accountable	partner picked to help you stay committed to avoiding/overcoming each needless fear while working toward success (determined by you as part of your plan to succeed)
Realistic	each needless fear to avoid/overcome while working toward success is attainable, given your resources and within the time frame set by you
Time-bound	time frame established and committed to by you

As discussed in chapter 6, using the above system to Make All Your Successes SMART, create a SMART System Tracker that will keep you accountable for progress while living and practicing principle number 6: *do not fear failure while working toward success!* The SMART Tracker below will help you get started. Make your own SMART System Trackers to use on as many successes as you wish to achieve.

SMART Tracker

Avoid/Overcome Needless Fear while Working toward Success:

Specific	Progress	Week #	Result
Measurable	Progress	Week #	Result
Accountable	Progress	Week #	Result
Realistic	Progress	Week #	Result
Time-bound	Progress	Week #	Result

As discussed in chapter 6, at the top of the SMART Tracker (above), write in the Needless Fear to Avoid/Overcome while Working toward Success.

Use each of the SMART boxes to ensure that you avoid/overcome needless fear according to the SMART system (Specific, Measurable, Accountable, Realistic, and Time-bound).

In the Progress boxes, mark a "+" if you were on target and a "–" if you were not on target. This will help you stay accountable, whether you are doing this on your own or with a partner.

In the Week # boxes, just indicate which week it is, to help you stay accountable.

In the Results box, indicate the outcome of having avoided/overcome fear of failure while working toward success.

Repeat the above steps for as long as you need to until you achieve your desired result(s). After that, move to the next habit you wish to remove and follow the same steps. Make your own SMART System Trackers to use on as many successes as you wish to achieve.

Revisiting Helping Your Children with the SMART[13] System Tracker for Success

Principle #6: Do not fear failure while working toward success!

Help Your Children Make All Successes SMART!

Specific	images, quotes, words, etc., collected for each needless fear you choose to avoid/overcome while working toward success
Measurable	goal set for each needless fear you choose to avoid/overcome while working toward success
Accountable	partner picked to help you stay committed to avoiding/overcoming each needless fear while working toward success (determined by you as part of your plan to succeed)
Realistic	each needless fear to avoid/overcome while working toward success is attainable, given your resources and within the time frame set by you
Time-bound	time frame established and committed to by you

As discussed in chapter 6, using the above system to Make All Successes SMART, help your child(ren) create a SMART System Tracker that will keep all of you accountable for progress while living and practicing principle number 6: *do not fear failure while working toward success!* The tracker below will help you get your child(ren) started. Follow the same system you used to complete your own tracker(s), but in an age-appropriate way for your child(ren). Make your own SMART System Trackers to use on as many successes as you want your child(ren) to achieve.

SMART Tracker

Avoid/Overcome Needless Fear while Working toward Success:

Specific	Progress	Week #	Result
Measurable	Progress	Week #	Result
Accountable	Progress	Week #	Result
Realistic	Progress	Week #	Result
Time-bound	Progress	Week #	Result

[Author's Note: *The following instructions, which are the same ones that appeared with the tracker in the previous section, are designed for parents to use with their child(ren), in an age-appropriate way. They are not intended for children to use on their own.*]

As discussed in chapter 6, at the top of the SMART Tracker (above), write in the Avoid/Overcome Needless Fear while Working toward Success.

Use each of the SMART boxes to ensure that you avoid/overcome needless fear according to the SMART system (Specific, Measurable,

Accountable, Realistic, and Time-bound).

In the Progress boxes, mark a "+" if you were on target and a "−" if you were not on target. This will help you stay accountable, whether you are doing this on your own or with a partner.

In the Week # boxes, just indicate which week it is, to help you stay accountable.

In the Results box, indicate the outcome of having avoided/overcome needless fear while working toward success.

Repeat the above steps for as long as you need to until you achieve your desired result(s). After that, move to the next habit you wish to remove and follow the same steps. Make your own SMART System Trackers to use on as many successes as you wish your child(ren) to achieve.

Revisiting the SMART[14] System Tracker for Dreams/Goals

We explored how to make dreams/goals SMART in the introduction, and how to guide our children to do so as well. Let's briefly recap our discussion there:

We all may know it's important to have dreams and to fulfill them. But one of the most important lessons we parents can teach our children is how to dream smart—not just smart, but SMART (Specific, Measurable, Accountable, Realistic, Time-bound).[15] SMART dreams are easier to fulfill because they become goals. Realized goals become achievements, and attained achievements lead to lasting success and fulfillment. Understanding how to dream SMART shows children how to set and reach attainable goals, how to recognize the difference between a dream and a goal, and how to make dreams reality—if they are willing to do the work required to get there.

Remember, no one can set or reach a goal without first having a dream!

The pages that follow contain additional SMART System Trackers for Dreams/Goals to use as described in the introduction. The first one is a SMART Tracker for you to use to implement your own dreams/goals, and the other one is for you to use to help your child(ren) create SMART dreams/goals in age-appropriate ways. You can create as many additional trackers of this type as you need for future dreams/goals for you and your child(ren).

Make All Your Dreams/Goals SMART!

Specific	images, quotes, words, etc., collected for each dream
Measurable	goal set for each

	dream
Accountable	partner picked to help you stay committed to each goal
Realistic	each goal is attainable, given your resources and within the time frame set by you
Time-bound	time frame established and committed to by you

As discussed in the introduction, using the above system to Make All Your Dreams/Goals SMART, create a SMART System Tracker that will keep you accountable for progress while living and practicing the 7 principles. The SMART Tracker below will help you get started. Make your own SMART System Trackers to use on as many dreams/goals as you wish to realize.

SMART Tracker

Dream/Goal: _____

Specific	Progress	Week #	Result

Measurable	Progress	Week #	Result
Accountable	Progress	Week #	Result
Realistic	Progress	Week #	Result
Time-bound	Progress	Week #	Result

As discussed in the introduction, at the top of the SMART Tracker (above), write in the Dream/Goal.

Use each of the SMART boxes to ensure that you create a goal from your dream according to the SMART system (Specific, Measurable, Accountable, Realistic, and Time-bound).

In the Progress boxes, mark a "+" if you were on target and a "–" if you were not on target. This will help you stay accountable, whether you are doing this on your own or with a partner.

In the Week # boxes, just indicate which week it is, to help you stay accountable.

In the Results box, indicate the outcome of having created the goal from the dream.

Repeat the above steps for as long as you need to until you achieve your desired result(s). After that, move to the next dream you wish to turn into a goal and follow the same steps. Make your own SMART System Trackers to use on as many dreams/goals you wish to realize.

Revisiting Helping Your Children with the SMART[16] System Tracker for Dreams/Goals

Help Your Children Make All Dreams/Goals SMART!

Specific	images, quotes, words, etc., collected for each dream
Measurable	goal set for each dream
Accountable	partner picked to help you stay committed to each goal
Realistic	each goal is attainable, given your resources and within the time frame set by you
Time-bound	time frame established and committed to by you

As discussed in the introduction, using the above system to Make All Your Dreams/Goals SMART, help your child(ren) create a SMART Tracker that will keep all of you accountable for progress in achieving set goals. The tracker below will help you get your child(ren) started. Follow the same system you used to complete your own tracker(s), but in age-appropriate ways for your child(ren).

SMART Tracker

Dream/Goal: _____

Specific	Progress	Week #	Result
Measurable	Progress	Week #	Result
Accountable	Progress	Week #	Result
Realistic	Progress	Week #	Result
Time-bound	Progress	Week #	Result

[Author's Note: *The following instructions, which are the same ones that appeared with the tracker in the previous section, are designed for parents to use with their child(ren), in an age-appropriate way. They are not intended for children to use on their own.*]

As discussed in the introduction, at the top of the SMART Tracker (above), write in the Dream/Goal.

Use each of the SMART boxes to ensure that you create a goal from your dream according to the SMART system (Specific, Measurable, Accountable, Realistic, and Time-bound).

In the Progress boxes, mark a "+" if you were on target and a "–" if you were not on target. This will help you stay accountable, whether you are doing this on your own or with a partner.

In the Week # boxes, just indicate which week it is, to help you stay accountable.

In the Results box, indicate the outcome of having created the goal from the dream.

Repeat the above steps for as long as you need to until you achieve your desired result(s). After that, move to the next habit you wish to remove and follow the same steps. Make your own SMART System Trackers to use on as many dreams/goals as you wish your child(ren) to realize.

Using the SMART[17] System Tracker for Learning, Growth, and Healing

Do It SMART!

Specific	images, quotes, words, etc., collected for each area desired
Measurable	goal set for each area desired
Accountable	partner picked to help you stay committed in each area desired
Realistic	each area desired is attainable, given your resources and within the time frame set by you
Time-bound	time frame established and committed to by you

This is a blank SMART Tracker for you to use in any area(s) you choose.

SMART Tracker

Area Desired: _____

Specific	Progress	Week #	Result
Measurable	**Progress**	**Week #**	**Result**
Accountable	**Progress**	**Week #**	**Result**

Realistic	Progress	Week #	Result

Time-bound	Progress	Week #	Result

As explained previously, at the top of the SMART Tracker (above), write in the Area Desired. This can be anything you wish to learn more about, grow in or from, or heal.

Use each of the SMART boxes to ensure that you examine each area desired according to the SMART system (Specific, Measurable, Accountable, Realistic, and Time-bound).

In the Progress boxes, mark a "+" if you were on target and a "–" if you were not on target. This will help you stay accountable, whether you are doing this on your own or with a partner.

In the Week # boxes, just indicate which week it is, to help you stay accountable.

In the Results box, indicate the outcome of examining each area desired.

Repeat the above steps for as long as you need to until you achieve your desired result(s). After that, move to the next area desired and follow the same steps. Make your own SMART System Trackers to use on as many areas desired as you wish to explore.

Helping Your Children with the SMART[18] System Tracker for Learning, Growth, and Healing

Help Your Children Do It SMART!

Specific	images, quotes, words, etc., collected for each area desired
Measurable	goal set for each area desired
Accountable	partner picked to help you stay committed in each area desired
Realistic	each area desired is attainable, given your resources and within the time frame set by you
Time-bound	time frame established and committed to by you

This is a blank SMART Tracker for you to use in any area(s) you and your child(ren) choose.

SMART Tracker

Area Desired: _____

Specific	Progress	Week #	Result
Measurable	Progress	Week #	Result
Accountable	Progress	Week #	Result

Realistic	Progress	Week #	Result
Time-bound	Progress	Week #	Result

[Author's Note: *The following instructions, which are the same ones that appeared with the tracker in the previous section, are designed for parents to use with their child(ren), in an age-appropriate way. They are not intended for children to use on their own.*]

As explained previously, at the top of the SMART Tracker (above), write in the Area Desired. This can be anything you wish to learn more about, grow in or from, or heal.

Use each of the SMART boxes to ensure that you examine each area desired according to the SMART system (Specific, Measurable, Accountable, Realistic, and Time-bound).

In the Progress boxes, mark a "+" if you were on target and a "–" if you were not on target. This will help you stay accountable, whether you are doing this on your own or with a partner.

In the Week # boxes, just indicate which week it is, to help you stay accountable.

In the Results box, indicate the outcome of examining each area desired.

Repeat the above steps for as long as you need to until you achieve your desired result(s). After that, move to the next area desired and follow the same steps. Make your own SMART System Trackers to use on as many areas desired as you and your child(ren) wish to explore.

Now that we've revisited the "Principles in Practice" and the "SMART System," let's move on to the next tool in our arsenal of faith-based living: using the technique of guided journaling.

In the Guided Journaling pages that follow, you will be able to more deeply explore your thoughts and feelings about the 7 principles and the scripture verses discussed throughout this book. There are also Guided Journaling pages for you to use with your child(ren), in age-appropriate ways.

Guided Journaling

As described, guided journaling is an effective technique for more deeply exploring thoughts and feelings on specific topics.

In the Guided Journaling pages that follow, there will be pages for each of the 7 principles and for each of the scripture verses that open the chapters and the conclusion (including what faith-based living/parenting means to you). These will appear consecutively, matching the flow throughout the book's chapters.

Following each set of pages for you to use yourself, there will be Guided Journaling pages for you to use with your child(ren), in age-appropriate ways. There will be a page for each of the 7 principles and for each of the scripture verses that open the chapters and the conclusion (including what it means to your child to live in faith). Here again, these will appear consecutively, matching the flow throughout the book's chapters.

Guided Journaling—For Parents

What does principle number 1—*seek the truth, and base your life on it*—mean to you?

_____

_____

_____

_____

_____

_____

_____

_____

_____

_____

_____

_____

_____

_____

_____

_____

_____

_____

_____

Guided Journaling—For Parents

What does the scripture verse we explored in this chapter—"Show me your ways, LORD, teach me your paths. Guide me in your truth and teach me, for you are God my Savior, and my hope is in you all day long" (Psalm 25:4–5 NIV)—mean to you?

_____

_____

_____

_____

_____

_____

_____

_____

_____

_____

_____

_____

_____

_____

_____

_____

_____

_____

_____

_____

Guided Journaling—For Children

Now that we've talked about it some more, what do you think it means to seek the truth, and base your life on it? Let's write down your thoughts and feelings about this:

_____

_____

_____

_____

_____

_____

_____

_____

_____

_____

_____

_____

_____

_____

_____

_____

_____

_____

Guided Journaling—For Children

Let's also talk about a scripture verse: "Show me your ways, LORD, teach me your paths. Guide me in your truth and teach me, for you are God my Savior, and my hope is in you all day long" (Psalm 25:4–5 NIV).

What do those words mean to you? How can we help God to teach us better and guide us better to live in truth? Let's write down your thoughts and feelings about this:

_____

_____

_____

_____

_____

_____

_____

_____

_____

_____

_____

_____

_____

_____

_____

Guided Journaling—For Parents

What does principle number 2—*understand who you are by knowing your family history and traditions*—mean to you?

_____

_____

_____

_____

_____

_____

_____

_____

_____

_____

_____

_____

_____

_____

_____

_____

_____

_____

Guided Journaling—For Parents

What does the scripture verse we explored in this chapter mean to you? "For the promise is unto you, and to your children, and to all that are afar off, [even] as many as the LORD our God shall call" (Acts 2:39 KJV).

_____

_____

_____

_____

_____

_____

_____

_____

_____

_____

_____

_____

_____

_____

_____

_____

Guided Journaling—For Children

We've talked about it a bit, so what do you think it means to understand who you are by knowing your family history and traditions? Let's write down your thoughts and feelings about this:

_____

_____

_____

_____

_____

_____

_____

_____

_____

_____

_____

_____

_____

_____

_____

_____

_____

_____

_____

Guided Journaling—For Children

Let's also talk about a scripture verse: "For the promise is unto you, and to your children, and to all that are afar off, [even] as many as the LORD our God shall call" (Acts 2:39 KJV).

What do those words mean to you? How can we keep this promise to God? Let's write down your thoughts and feelings about this:

_____

_____

_____

_____

_____

_____

_____

_____

_____

_____

_____

_____

_____

_____

Guided Journaling—For Parents

What does principle number 3—*be family oriented*—mean to you?

_____

_____

_____

_____

_____

_____

_____

_____

_____

_____

_____

_____

_____

_____

_____

_____

_____

_____

_____

_____

_____

Guided Journaling—For Parents

What does the scripture verse (Psalm 127:3–5 NLT) explored in this chapter mean to you? Especially "Children are a gift from the LORD; they are a reward from him":

_____

_____

_____

_____

_____

_____

_____

_____

_____

_____

_____

_____

_____

_____

_____

_____

_____

_____

_____

Guided Journaling—For Children

Why is family important? Which is more important, our "real" family that we are related to or our friends who feel like family? Why? What is the difference between the two? Write down your thoughts and feelings about this:

_____

_____

_____

_____

_____

_____

_____

_____

_____

_____

_____

_____

_____

_____

_____

Guided Journaling—For Children

Let's also talk about a scripture verse (Psalm 127:3 NLT): "Children are a gift from the LORD; they are a reward from him."

What do those words mean to you? How do you think God wants us to use his gifts and rewards? Let's write down your thoughts and feelings about this:

_____

_____

_____

_____

_____

_____

_____

_____

_____

_____

_____

_____

_____

_____

_____

_____

Guided Journaling—For Parents

What does principle number 4—*be selective about your friends*—mean to you?

_____

_____

_____

_____

_____

_____

_____

_____

_____

_____

_____

_____

_____

_____

_____

_____

_____

_____

Guided Journaling—For Parents

What does the scripture verse we explored in this chapter mean to you? "He that walketh with wise [men] shall be wise: but a companion of fools shall be destroyed" (Proverb 13:20 KJV):

_____

_____

_____

_____

_____

_____

_____

_____

_____

_____

_____

_____

_____

_____

_____

_____

Guided Journaling—For Children

What do you think it means to *be selective about your friends*? Let's write down your thoughts and feelings about this:

_____

_____

_____

_____

_____

_____

_____

_____

_____

_____

_____

_____

_____

_____

_____

_____

_____

_____

_____

Guided Journaling—For Children

Let's talk about this scripture verse: "He that walketh with wise [men] shall be wise: but a companion of fools shall be destroyed" (Proverb 13:20 KJV).

What do you think that means? What do you think God wants us to do with the wisdom he gives us? Let's write down your thoughts and feelings about this:

_____

_____

_____

_____

_____

_____

_____

_____

_____

_____

_____

_____

_____

_____

Guided Journaling—For Parents

What does principle number 5—*change what you need to by removing bad habits*—mean to you?

_____

_____

_____

_____

_____

_____

_____

_____

_____

_____

_____

_____

_____

_____

_____

_____

_____

_____

Guided Journaling—For Parents

What does the scripture verse we explored in this chapter mean to you? "To put off your old self, which belongs to your former manner of life and is corrupt through deceitful desires, and to be renewed in the spirit of your minds, and to put on the new self, created after the likeness of God in true righteousness and holiness" (Ephesians 4:22–24 ESV).

_____

_____

_____

_____

_____

_____

_____

_____

_____

_____

_____

_____

_____

_____

_____

_____

_____

Guided Journaling—For Children

What do you think it means to *change what you need to by removing bad habits*? Let's write down your thoughts and feelings about this:

_____

_____

_____

_____

_____

_____

_____

_____

_____

_____

_____

_____

_____

_____

_____

_____

_____

_____

_____

_____

_____

Guided Journaling—For Children

Let's talk about this scripture verse: "To put off your old self, which belongs to your former manner of life and is corrupt through deceitful desires, and to be renewed in the spirit of your minds, and to put on the new self, created after the likeness of God in true righteousness and holiness" (Ephesians 4:22–24 ESV).

What do you think it means? How does God renew us in mind and spirit? Let's write down your thoughts and feelings about this:

_____

_____

_____

_____

_____

_____

_____

_____

_____

_____

_____

_____

_____

_____

Guided Journaling—For Parents

What does principle number 6—*do not fear failure while working toward success!*—mean to you?

_____

_____

_____

_____

_____

_____

_____

_____

_____

_____

_____

_____

_____

_____

_____

_____

Guided Journaling—For Parents

What does the scripture verse we explored in this chapter mean to you? "But let him ask in faith, with no doubting, for the one who doubts is like a wave of the sea that is driven and tossed by the wind. For that person must not suppose that he will receive anything from the Lord ..." (James 1:6–7 ESV).

_____

_____

_____

_____

_____

_____

_____

_____

_____

_____

_____

_____

_____

_____

_____

_____

_____

_____

Guided Journaling—For Children

Always remember that "if at first you don't succeed, try, try again!" Trying takes you at least halfway to success. As long as you know you tried your hardest and did your best, you have not failed, so *do not fear failure while working toward success!* So now, what do you think you can do to succeed without being afraid that you might not do as well as you hope you will?

Let's write down your thoughts and feelings about this:

_____

_____

_____

_____

_____

_____

_____

_____

_____

_____

_____

_____

_____

_____

_____

_____

_____

_____

Guided Journaling—For Children

Let's talk about this scripture verse: "But let him ask in faith, with no doubting, for the one who doubts is like a wave of the sea that is driven and tossed by the wind. For that person must not suppose that he will receive anything from the Lord ..." (James 1:6–7 ESV).

What do you think it means? How do you think God wants us to use our faith? Let's write down your thoughts and feelings about this:

_____

_____

_____

_____

_____

_____

_____

_____

_____

_____

_____

_____

_____

_____

_____

_____

Guided Journaling—For Parents

What does principle number 7—*always be yourself, but also see yourself as others see you*—mean to you?

_____

_____

_____

_____

_____

_____

_____

_____

_____

_____

_____

_____

_____

_____

_____

_____

_____

_____

Guided Journaling—For Parents

What does the scripture verse we explored in this chapter mean to you? "And be not conformed to this world: but be ye transformed by the renewing of your mind, that ye may prove what [is] that good, and acceptable, and perfect, will of God" (Romans 12:2 KJV).

_____

_____

_____

_____

_____

_____

_____

_____

_____

_____

_____

_____

_____

_____

_____

_____

_____

Guided Journaling—For Children

What do you think this means to *always be yourself, but also see yourself as others see you*? Let's write down your thoughts and feelings about this:

_____

_____

_____

_____

_____

_____

_____

_____

_____

_____

_____

_____

_____

_____

_____

_____

_____

_____

_____

Guided Journaling—For Children

Let's talk about this scripture verse: "And be not conformed to this world: but be ye transformed by the renewing of your mind, that ye may prove what [is] that good, and acceptable, and perfect, will of God" (Romans 12:2 KJV).

What do you think it means? How do you think God wants us to transform so that we can do his will? Let's write down your thoughts and feelings about this:

_____

_____

_____

_____

_____

_____

_____

_____

_____

_____

_____

_____

_____

_____

_____

_____

_____

Guided Journaling—For Parents

What does it mean to you to follow all 7 principles and to model faith-based living for your children?

_____

_____

_____

_____

_____

_____

_____

_____

_____

_____

_____

_____

_____

_____

_____

_____

_____

_____

Guided Journaling—For Parents

What does the scripture verse opening the conclusion mean to you? "I can do all things through him who strengthens me" (Philippians 4:13 ESV).

_____

_____

_____

_____

_____

_____

_____

_____

_____

_____

_____

_____

_____

_____

_____

_____

Guided Journaling—For Children

What do you think it means to love God and to live in faith? Let's write down your thoughts and feelings about this:

_____

_____

_____

_____

_____

_____

_____

_____

_____

_____

_____

_____

_____

_____

_____

_____

_____

_____

Guided Journaling—For Children

Let's talk about this scripture verse: "I can do all things through him who strengthens me" (Philippians 4:13 ESV).

What do you think it means? How do you think God strengthens us to do what he intends for us to do? Let's write down your thoughts and feelings about this:

_____

_____

_____

_____

_____

_____

_____

_____

_____

_____

_____

_____

_____

_____

_____

That brings us to the end of the Guided Journaling pages. I hope you have found the technique of guided journaling beneficial and meaningful and that you will use it ongoing for yourself and with your child(ren).

I also hope you will turn to the exercises and resources in this "Tools for Success" section time and time again for inspiration, encouragement, and reinforcement of the ideals and values I know we share as Christians and parents. May this book help you raise children as happy and successful as my wife's and my three daughters are!

Next you'll find the "References and Resources" section, which provides recommendations for inspiration and information that you can access as you choose.

References and Resources

The first resource I recommend, beyond any other, is the Holy Bible. Use whichever version(s) you prefer, in print or online. My preferred versions appear throughout this book, as notated in each verse of scripture cited.

Books

Carroll, P. *Win Forever: Live, Work, and Play like a Champion.* New York: Portfolio/Penguin Group, 2010.

Doran, G. T. "There's a SMART Way to Write Management's Goals and Objectives." *Management Review* 70, no. 11 (AMA Forum, 1981): 35–6. http://www.ncdhhs.gov/humanresources/pms/pm/smart.pdf.

Gladwell, M. *Outliers: The Story of Success.* New York: Back Bay Books/HBG, 2011.

Hayes, N. *When the Game Stands Tall: the Story of the De La Salle Spartans and Football's Longest Winning Streak.* Berkeley, CA: Frog, Ltd., 2003.

Jakes, T. D. *He-Motions: Even Strong Men Struggle.* New York: Putnam, 2004.

Kelly, M. *Dream Manager.* New York: Hyperion, 2007.

_____. *Greater Than Yourself: the Ultimate Lesson of True Leadership.* New York: Doubleday, 2009.

Kramer, G. *Stillpower: Excellence with Ease in Sports and Life.* New York: Atria Books/Beyond Words, 2012.

Marx, J. *Season of Life: A Football Star, a Boy, a Journey to Manhood.* New York: Simon & Schuster, 2004.

Meyer, P. J. "What Would You Do If You Knew You Couldn't Fail? Creating SMART Goals," in *Attitude Is Everything: If You Want to Succeed above and Beyond.* Waco, TX: Meyer Resource Group, 2003.

Osteen, J. *Breakout! 5 Keys to Go beyond Your Barriers and Live an Extraordinary Life.* Nashville, TN: FaithWords, 2013.

Music

"Lean on Me" by Kirk Franklin

"Take Me to the King" by Tamela Mann

Made in the USA
Monee, IL
05 July 2022